DATE DUE

A FIREFLY BOOK

Published by Firefly Books Ltd. 2005

Copyright © 2005 Edizioni Gribaudo, Savigliano (CN), Italy

First printing

Publisher Cataloging-in-Publication Data (U.S.)

Schuster, Cristina del Valle.
   Public toilet design : from hotels, bars, restaurants, civic buildings and businesses worldwide/ Cristina del Valle Schuster.
[288] p. : col. photos. ;   cm.
Summary: A guide to the design of over 80 public toilets, including materials and accessories used, construction techniques and lighting concerns. Also a section on the history and evolution of the public toilet.
ISBN 1-55407-119-4 (pbk.)
1. Public comfort stations—Planning. 2. Public comfort stations - History. I. Title.
628.4/5 dc22   RA607.S47 2005

Library and Archives Canada Cataloguing in Publication

Schuster, Cristina del Valle, 1979-
   Public toilet design : from hotels, bars, restaurants, civic buildings and businesses worldwide / Cristina del Valle Schuster.
ISBN 1-55407-119-4

1. Public comfort stations--Design and construction.
2. Public buildings—Toilet facilities—Design and construction.
3. Restrooms--Design and construction. I. Title.

RA607.S43 2005   725'.73   C2005-903218-9

Published in the United States by
Firefly Books (U.S.) Inc.
P.O. Box 1338, Ellicott Station
Buffalo, New York 14205

Published in Canada by
Firefly Books Ltd.
66 Leek Crescent
Richmond Hill, Ontario L4B 1H1

Printed in Italy

Editor and Texts
Cristina del Valle Schuster

Translation
Matthew Clarke (English text)
Maurizio Siliato (Italian text)
Jean-Pierre Layre (French text)
Marja Terpstra/Textcase (Dutch text)

Design and layout
Anna Soler

Editorial Project
Bookslab SL

Copy editing
Alessandro Orsi

PUBLIC TOILET DESIGN

From Hotels, Bars, Restaurants, Civic Buldings and Buinesses Worldwide

Cristina del Valle Schuster

FIREFLY BOOKS

CONTENTS

Most people do not like talking about their bodily functions, and bathrooms have traditionally been relegated to a secondary position as far as the design of public spaces is concerned. Public toilets are generally associated with cold, often anti-hygienic spaces that foment delinquency, perversion and vandalism. Nevertheless, bathrooms not only form part of our everyday life but also reflect the evolution of our hygiene, as well as expressing our cultural identities to such an extent that they form part of the history of civilization.

In recent years, bathrooms have been subject to greater attention on the part of designers, who give full rein to their creativity to turn bathrooms into an experience for the senses imbued with great artistic value. This book presents a selection of very diverse projects in which bathrooms enjoy a special status as a vehicle for emotions, various artistic and cultural expressions, corporate values and the requirements of different social groups. Particular attention has been paid to the latter, as the needs of a male user are not the same as those of a woman, child, senior citizen or handicapped person – and the design of a lavatory must take these characteristics into account. Over the course of four chapters – Leisure and Culture, Residential Bathrooms, Working Environment and Commuting Spaces – follows a global survey of bathrooms belonging to different types of buildings, including bars, restaurants, theaters, gyms, offices, hospitals, kindergartens, public institutions, airports and train stations, with special emphasis on the means used to bring together creativity and functionality.

It seems that designers are gradually rebelling against the taboos which dictate when, where, how and with whom we should relieve ourselves, and are converting a visit to the bathroom into not just a satisfaction of physical needs but also a pleasant experience.

La maggior parte delle persone si mostra reticente nel parlare delle proprie esigenze corporali, e per tradizione la stanza da bagno è stata relegata a un posto di secondo ordine per quanto riguarda il design e la progettazione di spazi pubblici. In genere, i servizi pubblici si associano a spazi freddi e spesso antigienici che sono teatro di abitudini perverse e atti vandalici. Ciò nonostante, il bagno fa parte non solo della storia della civiltà, ma anche della nostra vita quotidiana; è inoltre simbolo di identità culturale e dell'evoluzione delle nostre abitudini igieniche.

Negli ultimi tempi, il bagno è stato oggetto di un'attenzione sempre maggiore da parte di architetti e designer che danno libero sfogo alla loro creatività trasformando il sanitario in un'autentica esperienza per i sensi, impregnata di un alto valore artistico. Il presente volume raccoglie alcuni esempi di progetti molto diversi dove il bagno gode di una condizione privilegiata come veicolo di emozioni, espressioni artistiche e culturali varie, nonché di valori aziendali. Particolare attenzione è stata prestata inoltre alle esigenze dei vari gruppi di utenti: uomini, donne, bambini, persone anziane e disabili. Nel corso dei seguenti quattro capitoli – Leisure and Culture, Residential Bathrooms, Working Environment e Commuting Spaces – si effettua un percorso globale lungo bagni appartenenti a diversi tipi di edifici quali bar, ristoranti, teatri, palestre, uffici, ospedali, asili nido, istituzioni pubbliche, aeroporti e stazioni ferroviarie, sottolineando le soluzioni adottate in ogni progetto per fondere creatività e funzionalità.

A quanto pare vi è in corso una sorta di ribellione artistica da parte dei designer, intenti a sovvertire le regole e i tabù riguardanti l'uso di questi spazi pubblici – quando, dove, con chi, e in che modo, dobbiamo soddisfare le nostre esigenze fisiologiche. In questo modo la visita ai tanto vituperati gabinetti non è solo uno sfogo fisico ma diventa anche un'esperienza piacevole e amena.

La mayoría de las personas se muestra reticente al hablar de sus funciones corporales, y tradicionalmente el cuarto de baño ha sido relegado a un puesto secundario en cuanto al diseño de espacios públicos se refiere. Los servicios públicos se asocian generalmente a espacios fríos y frecuentemente antihigiénicos que favorecen la delincuencia, la perversión y el vandalismo. Sin embargo, el baño forma parte no sólo de nuestra vida cotidiana, sino que da fe de la evolución de nuestros hábitos higiénicos y expresa identidades culturales, de manera que forma parte de la historia de la civilización.

En los últimos tiempos, el sanitario está siendo objeto de una mayor dedicación por parte de los diseñadores, que dan rienda suelta a su creatividad para convertirlos en una experiencia para los sentidos e impregnarlos de un alto valor artístico. El presente libro recoge una muestra de proyectos muy diversos en los que el aseo disfruta de un estatus privilegiado como vehículo de emociones, expresiones artísticas y culturales diversas, valores corporativos y necesidades de colectivos distintos. A éstas últimas se les ha prestado una atención especial, puesto que no son iguales las demandas de un usuario masculino que las de una mujer, un niño, una persona mayor o un disminuido físico, grupos que el diseño del sanitario debe tener en cuenta. A lo largo de cuatro capítulos, Leisure and Culture, Residential bathrooms, Working Environment y Commuting spaces, se hace un recorrido global por lavabos pertenecientes a distintos tipos de edificios, que engloban bares, restaurantes, teatros, gimnasios, oficinas, hospitales, guarderías, instituciones públicas, aeropuertos y estaciones de tren, entre otros, con especial hincapié en las soluciones empleadas para fusionar la creatividad y la funcionalidad.

Parece que, poco a poco, los diseñadores se rebelan artísticamente contra los tabúes que dictan cuándo, dónde, con quién y de qué manera debemos aliviarnos, y convierten la visita al excusado no sólo en un desahogo físico, sino también en una amena experiencia.

Les gens parlent en général avec réticence de leur rapport avec les toilettes. La salle de bain a toujours de ce fait été cantonnée à un rôle secondaire lorsqu'il s'agit du design des espaces publics. Les toilettes publiques ont souvent été associées à des espaces froids et peu hygiéniques, lieux de délinquance, de perversion et de vandalisme. Ces endroits font cependant partie de notre vie quotidienne; ils témoignent de l'évolution de notre hygiène et expriment par là même nos identités culturelles. Ils font ainsi partie de l'histoire de la civilisation.

Au cours de ces dernières années, les designers sont intervenus plus fréquemment dans la conception des toilettes. Ils ont libéré leur créativité pour en faire des lieux agréables à dimension artistique. Ce livre nous montre des projets très différents dans lesquels les toilettes publiques accèdent à un statut privilégié: elles transmettent des émotions, des expressions artistiques et culturelles variées, des valeurs et des attentes liées aux différents groupes d'utilisateurs. Ces dernières ont fait l'objet d'une attention particulière, car l'utilisation qu'en font les hommes est différente de celle qu'en font les femmes, les enfants, les personnes âgées, les handicapés, autant de groupes humains que le design appliqué aux sanitaires doit prendre en compte. A travers quatre chapitres, Leisure and Culture, Residential bathrooms, Working Environment et Commuting spaces, on découvre des espaces de différents endroits - des bars, des restaurants, des théâtres, des clubs de gym, des bureaux, des hôpitaux, des garderies, des institutions publiques, des aéroports et des gares -, l'accent étant mis tout particulièrement sur les solutions employées pour fusionner créativité et fonctionnalité.

Aujourd'hui, les designers commencent à se rebeller contre les tabous qui dictent l'art et la manière d'aller aux toilettes. Cet instant n'est plus vécu comme un simple soulagement physique; ils la transforment en une expérience agréable et intéressante.

De meeste mensen hebben er moeite mee om over hun lichaamsfuncties te praten en het toilet komt van oudsher op het tweede plan bij het ontwerpen van openbare ruimtes. Openbare toiletten worden gewoonlijk geassocieerd met kille en vaak onhygiënische ruimtes die misdaad, perversie en vandalisme bevorderen. De wc maakt echter niet alleen deel uit van ons dagelijks leven maar is bovendien een voorbeeld van de evolutie van onze hygiënische gewoontes en culturele identiteit en maakt daarmee deel uit van onze beschavingsgeschiedenis.

De laatste tijd besteden ontwerpers steeds meer aandacht aan sanitair in hun design. Ze geven de vrije teugel aan hun creativiteit en veranderen wc's in een beleving voor de zintuigen met een hoge artistieke waarde. In dit boek staat een overzicht van zeer verschillende projecten waarbij het toilet een bevoorrechte plaats inneemt als overbrenger van verschillende emoties en artistieke en culturele expressies. Daarbij wordt vooral veel aandacht besteed aan de verschillende doelgroepen, aangezien de toiletwensen van een mannelijke gebruiker sterk kunnen verschillen van die van een vrouw, een kind, een ouder iemand of een lichamelijk gehandicapte. Een goede sanitairontwerper houdt rekeningen met alle verschillende behoeften. In vier hoofdstukken, Leisure and Culture, Residential bathrooms, Working Environment en Commuting spaces worden toiletten beschreven die deel uitmaken van verschillende locaties: bars, restaurants, theaters, sportscholen, kantoren, ziekenhuizen, crèches, luchthavens en treinstations. In de meeste gevallen wordt de nadruk gelegd op de oplossingen die zijn gevonden om creativiteit en functionaliteit met elkaar in evenwicht te brengen.

Het lijkt erop dat de ontwerpers zich langzamerhand losmaken van de regels die voorschrijven wanneer, waar en hoe wij onze behoeften dienen te doen. Toiletbezoek is daarmee niet langer alleen maar gericht op het fysieke, maar kan ook een leuk uitje worden.

LEISURE AND CULTURE

It is the premises devoted to entertainment that boast the most spectacular bathrooms. Designers and architects no longer consider a bathroom a secondary space but, on the contrary, have started to discover the creative potential offered by this room, generally of limited dimensions. It is maybe the latter factor that demands a concentration of solutions, while the element of spectacle implicit in the bathrooms in bars, restaurants, clubs and theaters, makes entering them seem like an immersion into a world of fantasy and imagination.

È negli spazi dedicati allo svago e all'intrattenimento che si trovano i bagni più spettacolari. Designer e architetti non concepiscono più le toilette come spazi secondari, ma al contrario iniziano a scoprire il potenziale creativo offerto da questi vani dalle dimensioni generalmente ridotte. Probabilmente, per via dei pochi metri quadrati a disposizione che obbligano a una concentrazione delle soluzioni, o alla componente scenografica implicita in questi ambienti, entrare nei bagni di bar, ristoranti, club e teatri è come tuffarsi in un mondo di fantasia e immaginazione.

Es en los espacios dedicados al entretenimiento donde se encuentran los lavabos más espectaculares. Diseñadores y arquitectos ya no perciben el sanitario como un espacio secundario, sino que, al contrario, empiezan a descubrir el potencial creativo que ofrece esta estancia de tamaño generalmente reducido. Quizá por sus escasos metros cuadrados, que obligan a una concentración de soluciones, o por los elementos escenográficos implícitos en estos espacios, entrar en los lavabos de bares, restaurantes, clubs y teatros equivale a sumergirse en un mundo de fantasía e imaginación.

C'est dans les espaces voués aux loisirs où l'on trouve les toilettes les plus spectaculaires. Les designers et les architectes ne les conçoivent plus comme des espaces de second rang, mais au contraire, ils commencent à découvrir le potentiel créatif qu'offrent ces endroits en général de petites tailles. C'est peut-être grâce à ces espaces réduits qui obligent à trouver des solutions concentrées ou à proposer implicitement de la qualité, qu'entrer dans les toilettes des bars, des restaurants, des discothèques et des théâtres équivaut à pénétrer dans un monde de fantaisie et d'imagination.

In de uitgaanswereld zijn de meest spectaculaire toiletten te vinden. Ontwerpers en architecten beschouwen sanitair niet langer als secundaire ruimte. Integendeel, ze beginnen de creatieve potentie van deze veelal kleine kamertjes te ontdekken. Misschien komt het juist door de beperkte afmetingen, die tot creatieve, onconventionele oplossingen aanzetten, dat je bij een bezoek aan deze ruimtes in bars, restaurants, clubs en theaters steeds vaker een verbeeldingsrijke fantasiewereld binnenstapt.

sKETCH

This bathroom's concept and design, complete with striking colors, sparkles and unusual forms, make it something special and raise it to the same level as the other areas of this bar. The designers have given free rein to their imagination by designing the women's toilets as if they were pearls inside a jewel box. Their pearl-gray contrasts with the explosion of bright reds used to decorate the men's toilets.

Il design e la concezione dei colori, delle forme singolari e scintillii vari elevano questo bagno alla categoria di spazio privilegiato, mettendolo sullo stesso piano degli altri spazi del locale. Dando libero sfogo alla loro immaginazione, i designer hanno progettato i bagni per le donne come se fossero perle all'interno di un portagioie; il colore grigio perla che li riveste contrasta con l'esplosione di rossi intensi che decorano il bagno degli uomini.

Colores, destellos y formas singulares elevan este lavabo a la categoría de espacio privilegiado por su concepción y diseño y lo ponen a la altura de los demás espacios del local. Dando rienda suelta a su imaginación, los diseñadores han proyectado los baños femeninos como si fueran perlas dentro de un joyero, el color gris que los recubre contrasta con la explosión de rojos intensos que decora el lavabo de caballeros.

Couleurs, éclats et formes originales transforment ces toilettes, par leur conception et leur design, en un espace privilégié, le mettant au même niveau que les autres espaces du lieu. Laissant libre cours à leur imagination, les designers ont conçu les toilettes féminines comme des perles dans un coffret à bijoux. La couleur gris perle qui les recouvre contraste avec l'explosion des rouges intenses qui décorent les toilettes masculines.

De kleuren, fonkelingen en bijzondere vormen van dit toilet maken het tot een bijzonder ontwerp dat even interessant is als de rest van de ruimtes van deze Londense bar. De ontwerpers hebben hun verbeelding de vrije loop gelaten. De damestoiletten lijken parels in een juwelenkistje. Het parelgrijs vormt een sterk contrast met de felle rode kleuren van de herentoiletten.

Architect: Mourad Mazouz
Photography: Red Cover
Location: London, UK

This bar in London shows perfectly how original a public bathroom can be.

Questo bar londinese dimostra perfettamente come anche un bagno pubblico possa essere estremamente originale.

Este bar londinense ilustra sin duda alguna lo original que puede llegar a ser un baño público.

L'exemple de ce bar londonien illustre sans aucun doute le côté original que peuvent revêtir des toilettes publiques.

Deze ontwerpers laten zien hoe origineel een openbaar toilet kan zijn.

CASA DÉCOR 2003

2003, the Year of Design. Barcelona was chosen as the venue for a highly varied program of activities to celebrate the centenary of FAD, including the organization of the annual Casa Décor. A Prima Studio designed public bathrooms of outstanding colorfulness and originality for this well-known promoter of design and decoration, which was once again held in one of the city's most emblematic buildings.

2003, anno del Design. In occasione del centenario del FAD (Foment des arts decoratives), noto centro di promozione del design e dell'architettura, Barcellona è stata lo scenario di un vasto programma di attività, tra cui la celebrazione della fiera annuale Casa Décor. Per questa rinomata istituzione culturale, che occupa l'edificio di un antico convento in stile gotico del XVI secolo, lo studio A Prima ha disegnato i bagni pubblici degli spazi espositivi, dotandoli di colore e originalità.

2003, año del Diseño. Con motivo del centenario del FAD, Barcelona fue el escenario de un extenso programa de actividades, entre ellos la celebración de la feria anual Casa Décor. Para este conocido centro de difusión del diseño y la decoración, enmarcado una vez más en un emblemático edificio de la ciudad, el estudio A Prima diseñó los baños públicos del recinto, espacio que destaca por su originalidad y su colorido.

2003, année du Design. A l'occasion du centenaire du FAD, Barcelone a été le théâtre d'un vaste programme d'activités, notamment la célébration de la foire annuelle Casa Décor. L'atelier A Prima a conçu les toilettes de ce célèbre centre de diffusion du design et de la décoration, situé une fois de plus dans un bâtiment emblématique de la ville, créant un espace qui se démarque par son originalité et ses couleurs.

Barcelona stond in 2003 het gehele jaar in het teken van design. De Catalaanse hoofdstad was het toneel van een groot scala aan designactiviteiten, waaronder Casa Décor. Voor deze bekende jaarbeurs voor design en decoratie ontwierp studio A Prima de toiletten, die opvielen door originaliteit en kleurgebruik.

Architect: A Prima
Year: 2003
Photography: A Prima
Location: Barcelona, Spain

The use of new materials and bold colors were the trademarks of that year's Casa Décor, a fondamental event for all professionals from the world of decorating, architecture and interior design.

L'utilizzo di nuovi materiali e un uso estensivo del colore sono stati i tratti distintivi di questa edizione di Casa Décor, un appuntamento ineludibile per tutti i professionisti del mondo dell'arredamento di interni, dell'architettura e della decorazione in genere.

El empleo de nuevos materiales y un uso extensivo del color son la tónica que ha marcado esta edición de Casa Décor, cita ineludible para todo profesional del mundo de la decoración, la arquitectura y el interiorismo.

L'utilisation de nouveaux matéraiux et l'emploi massif de la couleur ont marqué cette édition de Casa Décor, rendez-vous incontournable pour tous les professionnels du monde de la décoration, de l'architecture et du design intérieur.

De toepassing van nieuwe materialen en uitbundige kleuren was het tonicum van deze editie van Casa Décor, een belangrijke ontmoetingsplaats voor iedereen die werkzaam is in architectuur, design en woninginrichting.

YORK EVENT THEATRE

Lighting plays a decisive role in the design of the bathroom in this venue. Both men's and women's bathrooms are divided into three linked sections: a small entrance hall, a space for the washbasins and another for the toilets. The only difference between the toilets is the color scheme – black and white for the gents, bright red for the ladies.

L'illuminazione svolge un ruolo determinante nel design dei bagni di questa sala per conferenze ed eventi. Sia la toilette degli uomini che quella delle donne sono divise in tre parti comunicanti tra loro: un piccolo ambiente all'ingresso, uno spazio riservato ai lavabi, e un altro ai bagni. I due servizi si differenziano soltanto per il colore delle pareti: bianco e nero per i signori e rosso intenso per le signore.

La iluminación desempeña un papel determinante en el diseño de los baños de esta sala de eventos. Tanto el servicio de hombres como el de mujeres están divididos en tres partes comunicadas: un pequeño recibidor en la entrada, un espacio destinado a los lavabos y otro para los baños. Ambos servicios difieren únicamente en el color de las paredes tramadas, blancas y negras las de los caballeros, de un rojo intenso las de las damas.

L'éclairage joue un rôle essentiel dans le design des toilettes de cette salle de spectacles. Les toilettes des hommes tout comme celles des femmes sont divisées en trois parties qui communiquent entre-elles: une petite entrée, un espace destiné aux lavabos et un autre pour les toilettes. C'est la couleur des murs tramés qui différencie les espaces de chacun des toilettes: blancs et noirs pour les toilettes des hommes et rouge vif pour celles des femmes.

De belichting is een doorslaggevende factor in het ontwerp van het sanitair van deze evenementenhal. Zowel het heren- als het damestoilet is verdeeld in drie met elkaar verbonden delen: een kleine entree, een wastafelgedeelte en dan de kleine kamertjes. De twee afdelingen verschillen enkel qua kleur van elkaar, namelijk witte en zwarte strepen bij de heren en felrood bij de dames.

Architect: II by IV Design Associates
Year: 2002
Photography: David Whittaker
Location: Toronto, Canada

KABARET'S PROPHECY

The bathrooms of the Kabaret's Prophecy club are conceived as places for socializing and therefore transcend the normal functions of a toilet. Thanks to the work of the illustrator Jamie Hewlett, creator of *Tank Girl*, and the visual image of the musical group Gorillaz, the bathrooms create an atmosphere that is both glamorous and intimate. They are adorned with Hewlett's drawings, which show insolent young men and ultra-sexy females in suggestive postures.

I bagni del club Kabaret's Prophecy sono stati concepiti come un luogo di socializzazione, trascendendo pertanto le consuete funzioni tipiche di questi spazi. Grazie all'illustratore Jamie Hewlett, creatore del fumetto cult Tank Girl e dell'estetica del gruppo musicale Gorillaz, i servizi rispecchiano un ambiente affascinante e al contempo intimo. Il bagno è popolato da disegni di ragazzi irriverenti e di donne in atteggiamenti provocatori.

Los lavabos del club Kabaret's Prophecy están concebidos como lugar de socialización y transcienden así la habitual función del baño. Gracias al ilustrador Jamie Hewlett, creador de Tank Girl y de la estética del grupo musical Gorillaz, los servicios reflejan un ambiente a la vez glamouroso e íntimo. El baño está poblado por sus dibujos de chicos insolentes en posturas provocativas.

Les toilettes du club Kabaret's Prophecy ont été conçues comme un lieu de socialisation. Ils transcendent ainsi la fonction traditionnelle des sanitaires. Grâce à l'illustrateur Jamie Hewlett, créateur de Tank Girl et de l'esthétique du groupe musical Gorillaz, les toilettes reflètent une ambiance à la fois glamour et intime. Les toilettes sont décorées par ses dessins qui montrent des garçons insolents et des figures féminines ultra-sexys dans des positions provocatrices.

De wc's van de club Kabaret's Prophecy zijn bedoeld als ontmoetingsruimte en overstijgen daarmee de gemiddelde toiletfunctie. Dankzij de illustrator Jamie Hewlett, bedenker van Tank Girl en van de look van de muziekgroep Gorillaz, is dit sanitair tegelijkertijd *glamourous* en intiem. De wc wordt bevolkt door zijn opvallende creaties: brutale jochies en ultrasexy vrouwenfiguren die in provocerende poses zijn afgebeeld.

Architect: David Collins
Year: 2004
Photography: Adrian Wilson, Tim Jenkins
Location: London, UK

The daring texts dotting the walls of the bathroom are complemented by fragmented images of lips and legs, as well as young women oozing sensuality. Kabaret's Prophecy reasserts the importance of the bathroom as a design space, without which no bar or club would be complete.

Frammenti di labbra e gambe, di ragazze che sprizzano sensualità da tutti i pori, completano gli audaci testi sparsi qua e là sulle pareti del bagno. Kabaret's Prophecy rivendica l'importanza della toilette come spazio di design senza il quale l'estetica di un bar o di una discoteca non sarebbe completa.

Fragmentos de labios y piernas y chicas que rezuman sensualidad complementan los atrevidos textos que salpican las paredes del baño. Kabaret's Prophecy reivindica la importancia del lavabo como espacio de diseño sin el cual un bar o una discoteca no estaría completa.

Des fragments de lèvres et de jambes et des filles pleines de sensualité illustrent les textes osés inscrits sur les murs. Kabaret's Prophecy utilise le design pour souligner l'importance des toilettes, espace essentiel à l'intérieur d'un bar ou d'une discothèque.

Fragmenten van lippen en voeten en sensuele meisjes completeren de gewaagde teksten die de muren sieren. Kabaret's Prophecy beklemtoont het belang van het toilet als designruimte waar een hippe bar of discotheek niet meer zonder kan.

Section

LES T^ROIS GARÇONS

Entering this bathroom is like diving into the most typical era of the French rococò, as the name of this restaurant in London suggests. The toilet, and the white, marbled washbasin, match the exquisite white jugs arranged on a period table. The ensemble is completed by a series of objects from a variety of sources which, rather than clashing, create a delightful mixture of styles.

Entrare nel bagno di questo ristorante londinese vuol dire fare un passo indietro nel tempo e immergersi in un'atmosfera impregnata dal rococò più francese. La tazza WC e il lavabo in marmo bianco fanno pendant con i raffinati vasi disposti su un tavolo, anch'esso d'epoca. L'arredamento viene completato da una serie di oggetti appartenenti a periodi diversi che, anziché stonare, arricchiscono questa rigogliosa e originale mescolanza di stili.

Entrar en este lavabo equivale a sumergirse en la época del rococó más francés, como apunta el nombre de este restaurante londinense. El inodoro y el lavamanos de mármol blanco se corresponden con los exquisitos jarrones dispuestos sobre una mesa también de época. El conjunto se completa con una serie de objetos de diversas procedencias que, más que desentonar, hacen las delicias de tan exultante mezcla de estilos.

Entrer dans ces toilettes, c'est pénétrer dans l'époque la plus française du Rococco, comme le suggère le nom de ce restaurant londonien. Les toilettes et les lavabos en marbre blanc s'accordent aux magnifiques vases disposés sur une table, également d'époque. Une série d'objets de différentes provenances complète l'ensemble, se mariant à merveille au mélange des styles exubérants sans détonner.

Een bezoek aan dit toilet is als een duik in de Franse rococotijd, zoals ook de naam van dit Londense restaurant al aangeeft. De wc en de wastafel van wit marmer zijn in harmonie met de prachtige vazen die op een tafel uit dezelfde periode staan. Het geheel wordt gecompleteerd met een serie objecten in verschillende stijlen die niet detoneren maar juist voor een verfijnde finishing touch zorgen.

Architect: Noé Duchaufour-Lawrence
Photography: Red Cover
Location: London, UK

L O N D O N COLISEUM

After being closed to the public for several months, the London Coliseum reopened its doors with an enlarged ladies' bathroom, with double the previous capacity in order to avoid line-ups during the intervals. The washbasins are the outstanding features, as their whiteness and gentle forms endow them with the quality of sculptural objects. This project is classical, imbued with serenity for a mythical building on the London scene.

Dopo essere rimasto chiuso al pubblico per vari mesi, il London Coliseum ha riaperto le sue porte; i lavori di ristrutturazione hanno previsto anche l'ingrandimento dei bagni per le signore, i cui volumi sono raddoppiati al fine di evitare lunghe attese tra un atto e l'altro. Da notare i lavabi, il cui biancore e le morbide linee li rendono simili a oggetti scultorei. Un progetto classico pervaso di serenità per un mitico edificio londinese.

Después de estar cerrado al público durante varios meses, el London Coliseum ha reabierto sus puertas con la ampliación de los baños de señoras, cuya capacidad se ha doblado a fin de evitar colas durante los entreactos. Destacan los lavamanos, cuya blancura y formas suaves se asemejan a objetos escultóricos. Un proyecto clásico imbuido de serenidad.

Fermé au public pendant plusieurs mois, le London Coliseum a réouvert ses portes en agrandissant les toilettes pour femmes. Leur capacité a doublé afin d'éviter les files d'attente pendant les entractes. Les lavabos se démarquent par leur couleur blanche et leurs formes toutes en douceur. Ils ressemblent à des sculptures. L'ensemble classique dégage une sensation de sérénité dans ce bâtiment mythique du paysage londonien.

Na enige maanden gesloten te zijn geweest voor publiek heeft het London Coliseum zijn deuren weer geopend met een uitgebreid damestoilet. De oppervlakte is verdubbeld om lange rijen in de pauzes te voorkomen. Opvallend zijn de wastafels, die door hun blankheid en zachte vormen doen denken aan sculptuurobjecten. Een klassiek en sereen project voor een mythisch gebouw in het Londense uitgaansleven.

Architect: RHWL Architects
Photography: Grant Smith/View
Location: London, UK

CENTRAL LIBRARY ROTTERDAM

The refurbishment of this library in Rotterdam incorporates new bathrooms designed as free elements in space, surrounded by the light that shines through the glass walls, where the letters forming the Dutch word for "bathroom" are repeated. One bathroom is reserved for younger users, as you can see from the height of the toilets, each painted with a background of playful colors.

La ristrutturazione della biblioteca di Rotterdam ha inglobato i nuovi bagni come elementi liberi nello spazio, avvolti dalla luce irradiata dalle pareti di vetro, dove si moltiplicano le lettere che compongono la parola "bagno". Uno dei servizi è riservato esclusivamente agli utenti più piccoli, la cui età si intuisce dall'altezza a cui sono posti i WC, ognuno dipinto con uno sfondo di allegri colori.

La renovación de la biblioteca de Rotterdam incorpora los nuevos lavabos como elementos libres en el espacio y envueltos por la luz que irradian las paredes de cristal, donde se multiplican las letras que componen la palabra "lavabo". Un cuarto de baño se destina exclusivamente a los jóvenes usuarios, cuya edad se intuye por la altura a la que están situados los retretes, cada uno pintado con un fondo de colores lúdicos.

Les nouvelles toilettes conçues dans le cadre de la rénovation de la bibliothèque de Rotterdam s'intègrent dans l'espace comme autant d'éléments libres, éclairés par la lumière qui provient des parois en verre. Ces dernières reflètent les lettres du mot "toilettes". Un espace est exclusivement destiné aux jeunes utilisateurs, reconnaissable à la hauteur des urinoirs et peint avec des couleurs vives.

De renovatie van de bibliotheek van Rotterdam omvat onder andere nieuwe toiletten die als vrije elementen in de ruimte zijn geplaatst, omhuld door het licht dat op de glazen wanden straalt. Eén wc-ruimte is uitsluitend bestemd voor jonge gebruikers. De kleine potjes zijn stuk voor stuk in ludieke kleuren geschilderd.

Architect: Architectenbureau Van den Broek en Bakema
Year: 2004
Photography: Arjen Veldt Photography
Location: Rotterdam, the Netherlands

(-ten)(veroud.)kaptafel 2 (g.
vorm van toile(linnen,doek)] 1 (-ten)(veroud.)kaptafel 2 (g.
heeft of waarin hij of zij zich bij een bep. gelegenheid vertoont: *zij besteden veel g*
te toiletten, vgl. *avond*toilet, *bal*toilet 5 (-ten) wc (al of niet met wasgelegenheid
men bij het maken van zijn toilet nodig heeft. **toiletblok** (het) 1 (op campings e.d.
(m.); g.mv. het gaan naar het toil 5). **toiletgarnituur** (het), ste **toiletbenodig**
frouw (de (v.)), juffrouw die toezicht houdt in een toilet in een openbare gelegenheid en zorgt voor zeep, handdoeke
knappen. **toiletpapier** (het), closetpapier. **toiletpoeder** (het de (m.)) poeder. **toiletpot** (de (m.)), de pot van het
spiegel voor men toilet maakt, syn. *kapspiegel.* **toiletspons** (de), fijne spons die men g
eren en vervoeren van
men kleden: (ook wederk.) *zich*
toiletzak (de (m.))

The interior of each of the stalls making up the bathroom space resembles the four ludo chips that proclaim each player's color and creates a relaxed, cheerful setting.

Come i segnaposto colorati che identificano i vari giocatori del Trivial Pursuit, l'interno dei vari vani che ospitano i WC è contrassegnato da un colore diverso, il tutto all'insegna di uno stile spensierato e vivace.

Como las cuatro fichas del parchís que anuncian los colores esenciales de cada participante, se configura el interior de cada una de las piezas que integra el espacio del retrete, en una demostración de desenfado y viveza.

L'intérieur de chacune des pièces qui compose l'espace des toilettes a été conçu avec désinvolture en utilisant un jeu de couleurs différentes.

De levendige kleuren van het interieur van de toiletten corresponderen met de vier basiskleuren van de pionnen uit het mens-erger-je-niet-spel.

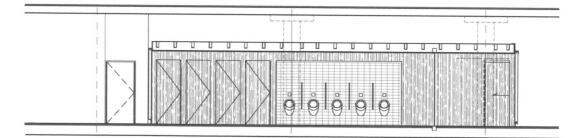

Section

SUPPERCLUB CRUISE

Supperclub Cruise arose from the desire to integrate a bar-club-restaurant inside a boat. Customers visit various places in the course of their partying in an approach that combines entertainment with the idea of a cruise. The bathrooms, set in a space flooded with bright red, contrast with the unremitting use of white in the main hall, and thereby provoke extremely different sensations.

Supperclub Cruise è la nuova Love Boat del divertimento, sorta ad Amsterdam all'interno di una nave da crociera. Tra danze e massaggi, i clienti di questo locale multifunzionale – bar, club e ristorante tutto in uno – possono cenare sdraiati su morbidi divani, circondati da uno spettacolo di musica, luci e ballerini. I bagni, immersi in uno spazio dal rosso intenso, contrastano con il candore delle pareti e dei soffitti *total white* della sala principale.

Supperclub Cruise nace de la voluntad de integrar un bar club y restaurante en el interior de un barco. Los clientes recorren en sus noches de fiesta distintos puntos geográficos, en una propuesta que combina el entretenimiento con el concepto de crucero. Los baños, inmersos en un espacio rojo fuertemente saturado, contrastan con el uso absoluto del blanco en la sala principal, experiencia que despierta sensaciones opuestas.

Supperclub Cruise regroupe un bar-club-restaurant à l'intérieur d'un bateau. Pendant les fêtes nocturnes qui sont organisées à bord, les clients voyagent en se promenant dans différents lieux géographiques. Deux concepts se mélangent, celui de la croisière et celui du divertissement. Les toilettes, situées dans un espace de couleur rouge vif, entrent en contraste avec la couleur blanche intense qui est utilisée dans la salle principale. L'ensemble provoque des sensations fortes.

Supperclub Cruise komt voort uit de wens om een barclub-restaurant op een boot te huisvesten. De bezoekers varen tijdens hun nachtelijke feestjes naar verschillende locaties, waarmee de Supperclub cruise echt een kruising is tussen uitgaanscentrum en pleziervaart. De toiletten, verzonken in een verzadigd rood, contrasteren met het gebruik van wit in de hoofdzaal, waardoor tegenstrijdige gevoelens worden opgeroepen.

Architect: Concrete Architectural Associates
Year: 2003
Photography: Concrete Architectural Associates
Location: Amsterdam, the Netherlands

 FIT^NESS HOTEL JUAN CARLOS I

The objects in this bathroom display a sculptural quality that converts this project into a space in which art strongly asserts its presence. From the basins to the ceiling lamps, from the ornamentation on the mirrors to the wrought iron decorating the central bench, each and every one of the pieces helps to create the sophisticated, elegant atmosphere that characterizes this luxury hotel.

Gli oggetti di questo bagno, dalla spiccata dimensione scultorea, trasformano questo progetto in uno spazio dove l'arte acquisisce una presenza più che palpabile. Dai lavandini fino alla lampade appese al soffitto, passando per la decorazione degli specchi e il ferro battuto che decora la panca centrale, tutti i singoli elementi contribuiscono a creare l'ambiente chic ed elegante che caratterizza questo hotel di lusso.

Los objetos de este baño poseen una dimensión escultórica que convierte este proyecto en un espacio donde lo artístico adquiere una presencia más que palpable. Desde las pilas hasta las lámparas que cuelgan del techo, pasando por la ornamentación de los espejos y el hierro forjado que decora la banqueta central, todas las piezas contribuyen a crear el ambiente chic y elegante que caracteriza este hotel de lujo.

Les objets qui composent ces toilettes ont une dimension sculpturale qui leur confère une portée artistique. Tous les objets contribuent à créer une ambiance chic et élégante, caractéristique de cet hôtel de luxe: miroirs, lampes qui pendent du plafond et fer forgé qui décore la banquette centrale.

De voorwerpen in dit toilet zijn zo prachtig van vormgeving dat er een bijna tastbare artistieke uitstraling van uitgaat. Van de wasbakken tot de lampen die aan het plafond hangen en de ornamentatie van de spiegels tot het gebruikte smeedijzer, alle delen dragen bij aan de totstandkoming van een chique en elegante ruimte die past in een luxe hotel.

Architect: Carlos Ferrater
Photography: Jordi Miralles
Location: Barcelona, Spain

The urinals are separated by translucent panels that provide intimacy without closing off the space.

Gli orinatoi sono divisi da pannelli traslucidi che donano intimità senza comunque chiudere lo spazio.

Los urinarios están separados por paneles translúcidos que proporcionan intimidad sin cerrar el espacio.

Les urinoirs sont séparés par des panneaux translucides qui offrent de l'intimité sans fermer l'espace.

De urinoirs zijn van elkaar gescheiden door lichtdoorlatende panelen die voor intimiteit zorgen zonder dat de ruimte wordt afgesloten.

JO S^HMO'S

A visit to the bathrooms of this restaurant resembles a trip back to the pop culture of the 1970s, with John Travolta and Olivia Newton-John looking down on the scene. An open space contains the bathrooms for both sexes, separated only by a stainless-steel frame. A blue light is used for the men's section, whereas the ladies' is pink. The results may be stereotyped but they do have a touch of chic sensuality.

Fare una visita ai bagni di questo ristorante equivale a fare un salto indietro nel tempo e tuffarsi nella cultura pop degli anni '70, sotto lo sguardo di John Travolta e Olivia Newton-John. Uno spazio aperto accoglie i servizi di ambo i sessi e i bagni veri e propri sono separati soltanto da un pannello di acciaio inossidabile. Una luce azzurra illumina la zona uomini, un'altra di color rosa quella delle donne, e il complesso risulta chic e sensuale.

Entrar en los baños de este restaurante es como sumergirse en la cultura pop de los años 70, con John Travolta y Olivia Newton-John observándolo todo. Un espacio abierto acoge los baños de ambos sexos y separa los lavabos únicamente con un marco de acero inoxidable. Una luz azul ilumina la parte de ellos, una rosa la de ellas, y el conjunto resulta chic y sensual.

Entrer dans les toilettes de ce restaurant, c'est pénétrer dans la culture pop des années 70, avec John Travolta et Olivia Newton-John comme toile de fond. Un espace ouvert accueille les toilettes hommes et femmes. Les lavabos sont séparés seulement par un panneau d'acier inoxydable. Une lumière bleue éclaire la partie des hommes et une lumière rose, celles des femmes. L'ensemble est chic et sensuel.

Wie de wc's van dit restaurant bezoekt, betreedt de popwereld van de jaren zeventig met John Travolta en Olivia Newton-John. In een open ruimte bevinden zich de toiletten van beide seksen die alleen van elkaar worden gescheiden door een roestvrijstalen frame. Blauwe lampen verlichten zijn deel, terwijl met een knipoog naar de "Pink Ladies" haar toilet in roze licht baadt. Hoewel stereotiep, heeft het geheel een chique en sensuele uitstraling.

Architect: Buckley Gray Yeoman
Photography: Chris Gascoigne/View
Location: London, UK

sPACE CONCEPTS 2001

In 2001, II by IV Design Associates designed an interpretation of a futuristic lifestyle, in an unconventional and minimalist theatrical setting, for the Interior Design Fair in Toronto. The most striking feature of the resulting prefabricated module was the use of multifunctional niches that serve as supports for mirrors, lighting systems and storage areas.

Nel 2001, in occasione della Fiera di Interior Design di Toronto, lo studio di architettura II by IV Design Associates ha interpretato uno stile di vita futurista in uno scenario teatrale minimalista e decisamente poco convenzionale. Un modulo prefabbricato il cui punto di forza principale risiede nell'utilizzo di nicchie multifunzionali che servono per sistemare specchi, sistemi di illuminazione, o possono essere utilizzati come aree di deposito.

En el año 2001, II by IV Design Associates concibió para la Feria del Diseño Interior de Toronto una interpretación de un estilo de vida futurista en un decorado teatral minimalista y muy poco convencional. Un paquete prefabricado, cuya baza principal reside en el empleo de nichos multifuncionales que sirven para colocar espejos, sistemas de iluminación que pueden ser utilizados como áreas de almacenamiento.

En 2001, II by IV Design Associates a imaginé pour le salon du Design Intérieur de Toronto un style de vie futuriste dans un décor théâtral minimaliste, très peu conventionnel. Cela donne un ensemble préfabriqué dont l'intérêt principal réside dans l'utilisation de niches multifonctionnelles qui servent à installer des miroirs et des systèmes d'éclairage et qui peuvent aussi être utilisées comme lieux de stockage.

In 2001 maakte II by IV Design Associates voor de beurs voor interieurdesign in Toronto een futuristisch ontwerp in een minimalistisch, onconventioneel theatraal decor. Het geprefabriceerde pakket bestaat uit multifunctionele nissen waar spiegels en lichtsystemen in kunnen worden opgehangen maar die ook dienst kunnen doen als opslagruimte.

Architect: II by IV Design Associates
Year: 2001
Photography: David Whittaker
Location: Toronto, Canada

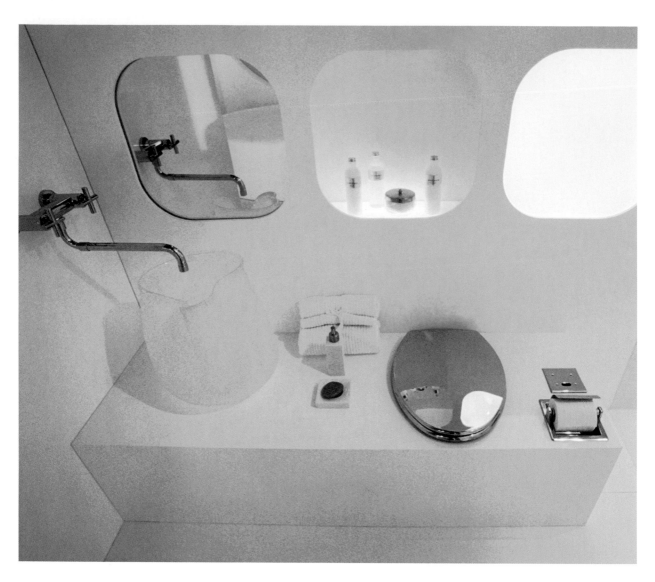

 Pristine white is the predominant element in this modern, flexible, sophisticated and highly functional space.

Il bianco puro è il protagonista assoluto di questo spazio moderno, flessibile, sofisticato e altamente funzionale.

El blanco puro es el protagonista absoluto de un espacio moderno, flexible, sofisticado y altamente funcional.

Le blanc pur est la seule couleur prédominante de cet espace moderne, flexible, sophistiqué et très fonctionnel.

Helderwit speelt de absolute hoofdrol in deze moderne, flexibele, geraffineerde en uiterst functionele ruimte.

 su**G**ar

The contrast between the preexisting brick wall and the use of new plastic materials defines the bathrooms of this Californian club. Plastic was chosen for its qualities of transparency and reflection, its range of translucence, its distorting effect and its saturation of color. Each bathroom is fitted with an acrylic door that provides a direct view of the toilet area.

Il contrasto tra la parete di mattoni già esistente e l'uso di nuovi materiali plastici definisce i bagni di questo club in California. La plastica è stata scelta per le sue qualità riflettenti, i suoi svariati indici di semitrasparenza, il suo effetto di deformazione e saturazione del colore. Ogni servizio dispone di una porta di acrilico che consente di vedere direttamente l'area dei lavabi.

El contraste entre la pared de ladrillo existente y la utilización de nuevos materiales plásticos define los baños de este club de California. El plástico se eligió por sus cualidades de transparencia y reflexión, sus variados índices de translucidez, su efecto de distorsión y la saturación del color. Cada uno de los servicios dispone de una puerta de acrílico que permite ver directamente el área de los lavabos.

Les toilettes de cette discothèque de Californie se caractérisent par l'utilisation de nouveaux matériaux plastiques qui contrastent avec le mur en brique existant. Le plastique a été choisi pour son effet de distorsion et ses propriétés de transparence, de réflexion, de translucidité variable et de saturation de la couleur. Toutes les toilettes disposent d'une porte en plastique acrylique qui permet de voir directement les lavabos.

Het contrast tussen de bestaande bakstenen muur en het gebruik van nieuwe materialen is karakteristiek voor de toiletten in deze Californische club. Het plastic is uitgezocht vanwege zijn transparante en reflecterende kwaliteiten en vanwege het vervormende effect. Ieder toilet beschikt over een deur van acryl waardoorheen je het wastafelgedeelte kunt zien.

Architect: John Friedman Alice Kimm Architects
Photography: Benny Chan/Fotoworks
Location: Santa Monica, USA

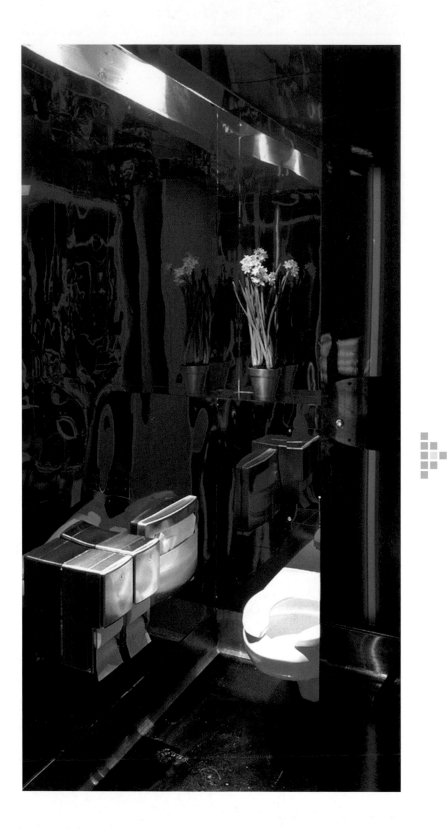

The walls and ceiling are covered with colorful acrylic panels, backlit by fluorescent tubes to give the space a sensual, all-embracing atmosphere.

Le pareti e il soffitto sono rivestiti da pannelli di acrilico colorati e retroilluminati da neon che danno allo spazio un'atmosfera avvolgente e sensuale.

Las paredes y el techo están cubiertos por paneles de acrílico coloreados y retroiluminados por fluorescentes que confieren al espacio una atmósfera envolvente y sensual.

Les murs et le plafond sont recouverts par des panneaux en acrylique colorés et rétro-illuminés par des fluorescents qui confèrent à l'espace une atmosphère envoûtante et sensuelle.

De muren en het dak worden bedekt door gekleurde panelen van acryl die met fluorescent licht worden belicht waardoor de ruimte een omhullende en sensuele atmosfeer krijgt.

COOLIE BASINS

The designers of the Avante UK group offered a new range of washbasins and faucets made in white marble and stainless steel, respectively. Their soft, round forms are contrasted with straight lines, evidence of a meticulous equilibrium that endows the space with a touch of cheerful minimalism and relaxed sobriety that make these basins suitable for any type of public space.

I designer del gruppo Avante UK propongono una nuova linea di lavabi e rubinetti realizzati rispettivamente in marmo bianco e acciaio inossidabile. Le forme morbide e arrotondate degli elementi si contrappongono alle linee rette, sfoggiando un accurato equilibrio che pervade l'ambiente di un allegro minimalismo e di una spensierata sobrietà, rendendolo adatto a qualsiasi tipo di spazio pubblico.

Los diseñadores del grupo Avante UK proponen una nueva línea de lavamanos y griferías realizados en mármol blanco y acero inoxidable respectivamente. Las formas suaves y redondeadas de los elementos se contraponen a las líneas rectas y hacen gala de un estudiado equilibrio que dota el espacio de un aire de alegre minimalismo y de una sobriedad desenfadada, volviéndolo adecuado a cualquier tipo de espacio público.

Les designers du groupe Avante UK proposent une nouvelle ligne de lavabos et de robinetterie fabriquée en marbre et en acier inoxydable. Les formes douces et arrondies des éléments s'opposent aux lignes droites. Il s'en dégage une sensation d'équilibre qui rend l'espace à la fois minimaliste et joyeux, sobre et serein. La ligne est adaptée à tout type d'espace public.

De ontwerpers van Avante UK komen hier met een nieuwe lijn wastafels en kranen van respectievelijk marmer en roestvrij staal. De zachte en ronde vormen van de elementen vormen een contrast met de rechte lijn, waardoor een weloverwogen balans wordt gecreëerd die de ruimte vult met een vrolijk minimalisme en onbevangen soberheid waarmee dit ontwerp geschikt is voor iedere openbare ruimte.

Architect: Avante UK
Photography: Red Cover
Location: UK

XL CHELSEA

The most eye-catching element in this project is an aquarium that runs round the entire perimeter of the space. This is a skillful ploy on the part of the designers, whereby visitors, instead of finding mirrors to give themselves a final touch-up before leaving the bathroom, encounter a relaxing underwater landscape that sends them on their way.

L'elemento di questo progetto che più attira l'attenzione è un acquario che lo percorre lungo tutta la superficie. Negli spazi che di solito accolgono gli specchi, usati per un ultimo controllo prima di uscire, i designer hanno deciso di collocare un acquario il cui rilassante paesaggio sottomarino accoglie e saluta gli utenti.

El elemento que más llama la atención de este proyecto es un acuario que recorre el espacio en todo su perímetro. Hábil sustitución la que han realizado los diseñadores, pues el lugar donde habitualmente se encuentran los espejos, que nos proporcionan una última comprobación de nuestro aspecto antes de salir del cuarto de baño, se convierte en un relajante paisaje submarino que despide al usuario.

D'emblée, ce qui attire l'oeil est un aquarium occupant toute la surface du lieu. Les designers ont habilement remplacé par un univers sous-marin apaisant ces miroirs qui nous renvoient d'habitude, à la sortie des toilettes, le reflet de notre propre image.

Het meest opvallende element in dit project is het aquarium. Een slimmigheidje van de ontwerpers, want op de plek waar gewoonlijk de spiegels hangen om ons een vluchtige blik op ons uiterlijk te gunnen voor we het toilet verlaten, bevindt zich nu een ontspannend onderwaterlandschap dat vriendelijk afscheid neemt van de toiletgebruiker.

Architect: Desgrippes Gobé Group
Year: 2001
Photography: John Horner
Location: New York, USA

ReSTAURANT
GEORGES AT THE CENTRE POMPIDOU

The bathrooms of this restaurant are located on the sixth floor of the Georges Pompidou Center, a very distinctive architectural context that designers have attempted to prolong. So, the Center's exposed pipes – the building's distinguishing trait – are recreated in the decoration of the bathrooms. The desire to intervene as little as possible in the preexisting architecture led the designers to work with the same material the floor is made of.

I bagni di questo ristorante si trovano al sesto piano del centro Georges Pompidou, un contesto architettonico molto peculiare che i designer hanno voluto conservare: il motivo dei tubi del Centro, tratto distintivo dell'edificio, viene infatti ripreso nelle decorazioni dei bagni. La volontà di intervenire il meno possibile nell'assetto architettonico già esistente li ha portati a lavorare con lo stesso materiale del pavimento.

Los lavabos de este restaurante se encuentran en el sexto piso del centro Georges Pompidou, un contexto arquitectónico muy peculiar que los diseñadores han querido continuar. La voluntad de intervenir lo menos posible en la arquitectura existente les ha llevado a trabajar con el mismo material del suelo.

Les toilettes de ce restaurant se trouvent au sixième étage du centre Georges Pompidou, un environnement architectural singulier que les designers ont cherché à souligner. Les tuyaux du centre, qui caractérisent le bâtiment, se retrouvent dans la décoration des toilettes. La volonté d'intervenir le moins possible sur l'architecture déjà existante a amené les designers à travailler avec le matériau utilisé pour le sol.

De toiletten van dit restaurant bevinden zich op de zesde verdieping van het Centre Georges Pompidou, een zeer bijzondere architectonische context die de wc-ontwerpers hebben willen continueren. Zo zijn de buisconstructies van het museum ook gebruikt in de decoratie van de toiletten. De wens om zo weinig mogelijk in te grijpen in de bestaande architectuur heeft de ontwerpers ertoe gebracht om hetzelfde materiaal te gebruiken als op de vloer.

Architect: Jakob + MacFarlane
Year: 2000
Photography: Nacása & Partners Inc.
Location: Paris, France

The floor becomes a new resource, as it is extended vertically and deformed to shape spaces containing the bathrooms.

Il pavimento diventa un nuovo campo di sperimentazione, estendendosi in senso verticale e deformandosi fino a generare dei volumi dove trovano spazio i bagni.

El suelo se convierte en un nuevo campo de experimentación. Al extenderse en sentido vertical y al deformarse, da lugar a volúmenes que dan cabida a los baños.

Le sol devient un nouveau champ d'intervention, qui s'étend à la verticale et se déforme pour créer des volumes qui agrandissent les toilettes.

De vloer gaat over in de verticale lijnen waardoor vervormingen ontstaan waarin plaats is ingeruimd voor de wc's.

BOIJMANS
VAN BEUNINGEN MUSEUM

The Boijmans Museum, situated in Rotterdam, chose this mobile unit for its public bathrooms to reflect the type of contemporary art put on show. They are situated outside the museum and stand out in the middle of the courtyard on account of the irregularity of their structure and their camouflage design. Inside, the acid green color creates an evocative space that sets off the curved forms of its elements.

Per i suoi bagni pubblici, il Boijmans Museum di Rotterdam ha optato per questa unità mobile che rispecchia la cultura dell'arte contemporanea esposta al suo interno. Situato fuori dal museo, il bagno si fa notare per la struttura irregolare e per i colori mimetici che spiccano in mezzo al patio. All'interno, il verde acido crea uno spazio suggestivo che mette in rilievo le forme curve dei suoi elementi.

El Boijmans Museum, situado en Rotterdam, escogió para sus baños públicos esta unidad móvil que refleja la cultura del arte contemporáneo que se exhibe en su interior. Situado en el exterior del museo, el baño destaca por la irregularidad de su estructura, con colores de camuflaje que resaltan en medio del patio. En el interior, el verde ácido crea un espacio sugerente que pone de relieve las formas curvas de sus elementos.

Le Boijmans Museum, situé à Rotterdam, a choisi pour ses toilettes publiques cette unité mobile. Elle symbolise la culture de l'art contemporain qui se dévoile à l'intérieur. Placées à l'extérieur du musée, les toilettes se détachent par l'aspect irrégulier de leur structure, camouflées sous des couleurs qui se remarquent au milieu de la cour intérieure. Dedans, l'espace a été peint en vert acide, une couleur qui souligne les formes arrondies des éléments.

Het Boijmans-van Beuningen Museum in Rotterdam heeft gekozen voor deze verplaatsbare openbare toiletten die de moderne kunst die er tentoon wordt gesteld weerspiegelen. De buiten het museum gelegen wc's vallen op door hun onregelmatige structuur en camouflagekleuren. In het interieur zorgt de gifgroene kleur voor een suggestieve ruimte die de gebruikte kromme vormen benadrukken.

Architect: Atelier Van Lieshout
Photography: Atelier Van Lieshout
Location: Rotterdam, the Netherlands

CINECITY TRIESTE MULTIPLEX

Who says that original public toilets are only found in bars and clubs? This bathroom, which belongs to a multiscreen movie theater complex, gives particular prominence to color and graphic design, creating a distinctive, youthful setting. Ingenious and amusing pictograms show the way through an acid-green tunnel that leads to the toilets assigned to ladies, gents and disabled people.

Chi dice che gli unici bagni pubblici originali si trovano soltanto nei bar e nei club? Questo bagno, all'interno di un cinema multisala, si affida al colore e alla grafica per creare uno spazio giovane e originale. Pittogrammi ingegnosi e divertenti indicano allo spettatore la strada da seguire lungo un tunnel di color verde acido che porta fino ai bagni per uomini, donne e persone disabili.

¿Quién dice que los únicos baños públicos originales se encuentran en bares y clubs? Este lavabo, perteneciente a un complejo de multicines, juega su baza más importante con el color y el grafismo para crear un espacio joven y original. Pictogramas ingeniosos y divertidos indican al espectador el camino que seguir por un túnel de color verde ácido que lleva hasta los baños de caballeros, damas y discapacitados.

Qui a dit que les seules toilettes publiques originales se trouvent dans les bars et dans les discothèques ? Les toilettes de ce cinéma multiplexe se distinguent par leur couleur et leur graphisme. Elles créent un espace jeune et original. Des pictogrammes ingénieux et amusants montrent au spectateur le chemin à suivre, un tunnel couleur vert acide qui conduit jusqu'aux toilettes des hommes, des femmes et des personnes à mobilité réduite.

Wie zegt dat originele wc's alleen te vinden zijn in bars en clubs? Dit toilet, dat deel uitmaakt van een bioscoopcomplex, speelt zijn belangrijkste troef uit met het gebruik van kleur en grafische kunst om een jonge en originele ruimte te creëren. Ingenieuze en grappige pictogrammen wijzen de filmbezoekers de weg door een gifgroene tunnel die leidt naar de toiletten voor dames, heren en gehandicapten.

Architect: Andrea Viviani
Year: 2003
Photography: Alberto Ferrero
Location: Trieste, Italy

The typeface and pictograms used in the bathrooms convey a fresh, modern image that corresponds with the young clientele they were designed for.

I caratteri e i pittogrammi utilizzati in questi WC trasmettono un'immagine di freschezza e modernità, consona al tipo di pubblico a cui sono rivolti.

La tipografía y los pictogramas utilizados en los inodoros transmiten una imagen de frescura y modernidad de acuerdo con el público joven al que van dirigidos.

La typographie et les pictogrammes utilisés dans les toilettes confèrent une image de fraîcheur et de modernité, en accord avec le public jeune auquel ils sont destinés.

De gebruikte typografie en pictogrammen in de toiletten dragen bij aan het frisse en moderne uiterlijk dat past bij het jonge filmpubliek.

sPAZIO A4

This club was designed as a large, multipurpose space that attempts to break free of stereotypes by creating a new relationship between the setting and the visitor. The bathrooms, which are reached via a curtain which replaces the conventional door, are preceded by an anteroom fitted with 13 computer screens that seem to observe the visitor's moves.

Questa discoteca è stata concepita come uno spazio volumetrico e polifunzionale dove, attraverso la creazione di nuovi rapporti spettatore-ambiente, si cerca di fuggire dagli stereotipi. I bagni, ai quali si accede attraverso una tendina che sostituisce la solita porta, sono preceduti da un'anticamera alle cui pareti sono stati incassati 13 schermi di computer, che sembrano osservare i movimenti del visitatore.

Esta discoteca está concebida como un espacio volumétrico y polifuncional que nace con la voluntad de huir de los estereotipos a través de la creación de nuevas relaciones espectador-entorno. Antes de llegar a los baños, a los cuales se accede a través de una cortina que sustituye a la puerta convencional, hay una antesala en cuyas paredes se han empotrado 13 pantallas de ordenador que parecen observar al espectador.

Cette discothèque est conçue comme un volume multifonctionnel, né de la volonté de fuir les stéréotypes en créant de nouvelles relations entre le spectateur et son environnement. On accède aux toilettes par un rideau qui remplace la porte conventionnelle. Elles sont précédées d'une avant-salle où 13 écrans d'ordinateur fixés au mur semblent observer le spectateur.

Deze discotheek is vormgegeven als een multifunctionele ruimte die is voortgekomen uit de wens om stereotypen te omzeilen met de creatie van een nieuwe relatie tussen bezoeker en omgeving. De wc's, toegankelijk via een gordijn dat de traditionele deur vervangt, worden ingeleid door een voorportaal waar 13 computermonitoren in de muur zijn gebeiteld, die de bezoeker lijken te observeren.

Architect: Simone Micheli
Year: 2004
Photography: Maurizio Marcato
Location: Piemonte, Italy

In these bathrooms black is the main color, only interrupted by the bright red on the mirrors and the cubicle doors.

Il colore che predomina in questi bagni è il nero, interrotto solo dal rosso vivo degli specchi e delle porte delle toilette.

El negro es el color dominante en los baños, sólo interrumpido por el rojo saturado de los espejos y de las puertas de los retretes.

Dans les toilettes, le noir est la couleur dominante mais elle est contrebalancée par le rouge des miroirs et des portes des cabines.

De dominante zwarte kleur in de toiletten wordt enkel onderbroken door het verzadigde rood van de spiegels en de deuren van de wc's.

SC**O**TTSDALE
MUSEUM OF CONTEMPORARY ART

This striking public building offers the citizens of Scottsdale a new gateway into the world of contemporary art. The bathrooms in this art gallery are in perfect visual harmony with the rest of the building, and share their desire to present a democratic view of art as a universal vehicle for emotions ever present in our everyday life…even when we go to the bathroom.

Grazie a questa singolare opera civica, la comunità di Scottsdale possiede un nuovo edificio dove mettere in mostra le ultime sperimentazioni e innovazioni creative di arte contemporanea. I bagni di questa galleria espositiva coesistono in piena armonia estetica con il resto dell'edificio, desiderosi di portare a termine la loro funzione democratizzante dell'arte come veicolo universale di sensazioni, presente in ogni momento della nostra vita quotidiana… persino quando si fa uso del bagno.

La comunidad de Scottsdale posee, gracias a esta singular obra cívica, un nuevo portal para experimentar con el arte contemporáneo. Los baños de esta galería de exhibición coexisten en plena armonía estética con el resto del edificio, ansiosos por llevar a cabo su función democratizadora del arte como vehículo universal de sensaciones, presente en todo momento de nuestra vida cotidiana… también cuando hacemos uso del baño.

La communauté de Scottsdale dispose avec cet espace d'une nouvelle plate-forme d'expérimentation de l'art contemporain. L'esthétique des toilettes de cette galerie d'exposition est en harmonie parfaite avec le reste du bâtiment. Elle parvient à donner à l'art sa vocation démocratique: transmettre des sensations universelles à tout instant de notre vie quotidienne… y compris dans des toilettes.

De gemeenschap van Scottsdale beschikt dankzij dit bijzondere initiatief over een nieuwe ruimte voor moderne kunst. De toiletten van deze galerie vormen een perfecte esthetische harmonie met de rest van het gebouw dat erop gericht is om de zinnen te begoochelen met moderne kunst, waar ook de toiletten een bijdrage aan leveren.

Architect: Will Bruder Architects
Year: 1999
Photography: Bill Timmerman
Location: Scottsdale, USA

RISTOTEATRO CENTRALE

The public bathrooms of this Italian theater are reached by going through a slightly curved transit area that is completely tiled with blue mosaic. A strong visual connection was sought with the elements inside the bathroom, such as the washbasin and the mirrors, so totally transparent materials and simple lines were chosen to capture light from the interior while also being fully integrated into the space.

Attraverso una zona di transito leggermente curva e interamente rivestita da un mosaico sull'azzurro, si accede ai bagni pubblici di questo teatro italiano. Al fine di stabilire un forte collegamento visivo con gli elementi dell'interno, come il lavabo e gli specchi, sono stati scelti dei materiali totalmente trasparenti, dalle linee semplici, in grado di catturare la luce dell'interno e al tempo stesso di integrarsi adeguatamente nello spazio.

A través de una zona de tránsito ligeramente curvada y revestida por completo de un mosaico azulado, se accede a los baños públicos de este teatro italiano. Quiso establecerse una fuerte conexión visual con los elementos del interior, como el lavamanos y los espejos. Para lograrlo se escogieron materiales totalmente transparentes y de líneas sencillas que captaran la luz del interior y se integraran, al mismo tiempo, en el espacio.

On accède aux toilettes de ce théâtre italien par une zone de circulation légèrement courbe et entièrement habillée d'une mosaïque bleue. On a voulu instaurer une forte connivence visuelle avec les éléments intérieurs, comme les lavabos et les miroirs. Des matériaux totalement transparents et aux lignes simples, capables de capter la lumière intérieure tout en s'intégrant à l'espace, ont été choisis pour obtenir cet effet.

Via een lichtgebogen gangetje dat geheel met blauw mozaïek is bekleed, kom je bij de sanitaire voorzieningen van dit Italiaanse theater. Het halletje is een duidelijke voorbode van de toiletruimte waarin transparante materialen en eenvoudige lijnen zijn gebruikt die samen met het licht voor een bijzonder effect zorgen.

Architect: Studio Gallucci
Photography: Matteo Piazza
Location: Rome, Italy

Particularly striking are the circular mirrors hanging above the central module, designed to ease the circulation.

Da notare gli specchi circolari appesi sopra un modulo centrale, che facilita la circolazione.

Destacan los espejos circulares suspendidos por encima de un módulo central que facilita el tránsito a su alrededor.

On remarque les miroirs circulaires suspendus au-dessus d'un module central qui rend la circulation plus facile.

Opvallend zijn de ronde spiegels opgehangen boven een centrale module waarmee de doorgang wordt bevorderd.

BLENDER

Colors and reflections join forces to create a surrealistic setting in these bathrooms. The bathroom doors and visitors' silhouettes are reflected, and grotesquely deformed, in the brass surface stretching along the entire corridor. The toilet cubicles, individually lit with their own color, combine together to create a rainbow effect.

Colori e riflessi uniscono le loro forze per creare nei sanitari di questo progetto un ambiente surreale. Le porte dei bagni e le sagome degli utenti vengono riflesse, e grottescamente deformate, sulla superficie di ottone che percorre tutto il corridoio. I cubicoli che contengono i WC sono dotati di un'illuminazione indipendente e di un colore proprio, che si combinano a creare un effetto arcobaleno.

Colores y reflejos aúnan sus fuerzas para recrear en los baños de este proyecto un ambiente surrealista. Las puertas de los retretes y las siluetas de los usuarios quedan reflejados y esperpénticamente deformados en la superficie de latón que se extiende a lo largo del pasillo. Iluminados cada uno con su propio color, los cubículos que acogen los inodoros recuerdan en conjunto a un arco iris.

Les couleurs et les reflets unissent leurs forces pour créer dans ces toilettes une atmosphère surréaliste. Les portes des cabinets et les silhouettes des utilisateurs sont reflétées et déformées sur la surface en laiton qui s'étend le long du couloir. Les couleurs différentes de chaque cabine, qui sont éclairées indépendamment, créent un arc-en-ciel.

Kleuren en reflecties zorgen in dit project samen voor een surrealistische uitstraling. De deuren van de toiletten en silhouetten van de bezoekers worden op groteske wijze vervormd in het messing oppervlak dat in de gang wordt gebruikt. Iedere toiletruimte wordt anders belicht waardoor een regenboogeffect ontstaat.

Architect: Concrete Architectural Associates
Year: 2000
Photography: Concrete Architectural Associates
Location: Amsterdam, the Netherlands

S.U.B. DISCOTEQUE

This original unisex module consists of four steel washbasins, each with a small mirror hung on it. Behind them lies the most intimate area, where there is a separation according to gender, indicated by means of pictograms and a different lighting scheme – pink for women and blue for men. The washbasins form an antechamber to this area that allows the two sexes to socialize.

Questo originale modulo unisex consta di quattro lavabi di acciaio sui quali pendono quattro piccoli specchi rotondi. Dietro si trova la parte più intima, dove alcuni disegni e un tipo d'illuminazione diversa – rosa e azzurra – identifica la zona riservata alle donne e quella riservata agli uomini. I lavabi sono concepiti come un'anticamera a questa zona e come spazio di socializzazione tra i due sessi.

Este original módulo unisex consta de cuatro pilas de acero sobre las que cuelgan cuatro pequeños espejos redondos. Detrás se encuentra la zona más íntima, donde la separación de sexos se indicada mediante pictogramas y una iluminación diferenciada – rosa para las mujeres y azul para los hombres. Los lavamanos se configuran como una antesala a esta área.

Ce module unisexe très original est composé de quatre vasques en acier au-dessus desquelles sont accrochés quatre petits miroirs ronds. La zone la plus intime se trouve derrière, endroit où il y a bien deux espaces distincts pour chaque sexe. La zone est indiquée par des pictogrammes et un éclairage différencié – rose pour les femmes et bleu pour les hommes. L'espace où se trouvent les lavabos sert en fait d'antichambre à cette zone; c'est un lieu de socialisation entre les deux sexes.

Deze originele uniseksmodule bestaat uit vier stalen constructies waar vier kleine ronde spiegels in zijn gemonteerd. Daarachter bevindt zich het meest intieme gedeelte, met aparte toiletten voor dames en heren, aangeduid door pictogrammen en verschillende soorten verlichting: roze voor vrouwen en blauw voor mannen. De wasbakken vormen het voorportaal van deze afgescheiden delen waar beide seksen elkaar ontmoeten.

Architect: Bolzen, Mehring & Partner
Photography: Jörg Hempel Photodesign
Location: Düsseldorf, Germany

CASA COR 2003

This exhibition space has set aside a minimalist, unisex bathroom for media workers. It contains three washbasins, four toilets but no urinal. The toilets are set in cubicles with glass walls covered by a translucent film. Video projectors throw images on to the front wall of these cubicles, turning them into large screens.

Questo spazio espositivo mette a disposizione dei vari utenti un bagno minimalista e unisex, composto da quattro gabinetti, tre lavabi e nessun orinatoio. Le tazze del water si trovano dentro cubicoli dalle pareti vetrate e ricoperte da una pellicola traslucida. Dei proiettori video tracciano immagini sulla parete frontale di questi cubicoli, trasformando le loro superfici in grandi schermi.

Este espacio de exhibición pone a disposición de los profesionales de los medios un baño minimalista y unisex. El lavabo se compone de cuatro retretes, tres lavamanos y ningún urinario. Los inodoros se encuentran dentro de cubículos de paredes acristaladas recubiertas por una película translúcida. Proyectores de vídeo trazan imágenes en la pared frontal de los cubículos y convierten sus superficies en grandes pantallas.

Cet espace d'exposition dispose de toilettes minimalistes et unisexes pour les professionnels des médias. On y trouve quatre W.C., trois lavabos et aucun urinoir. Les W.C. se trouvent dans des compartiments aux parois en verre translucide. Des projecteurs de vidéo passent des images sur les murs en face de ces compartiments et transforment leurs surfaces en grands écrans.

Deze tentoonstellingsruimte beschikt over een minimalistisch unisekstoilet bestaande uit vier potten, drie wastafels en geen urinoir. De kleine kamertjes zijn opgetrokken uit glazen wanden bedekt met een doorzichtig laagje waarop videobeelden worden geprojecteerd.

Architect: Marcelo Sodré
Year: 2003
Photography: Tuca Reines
Location: São Paulo, Brazil

The mirrors above the washbasins are no ordinary reflective surfaces but LCD screens that project images of the bathroom's users taken by hidden cameras. The effect is strange and slightly disturbing, although it contributes to a feeling of calm and luminosity.

Gli specchi situati sopra i lavabi non sono semplici superfici riflettenti, ma schermi LCD che proiettano immagini degli utenti ripresi da telecamere nascoste. L'effetto finale unisce un qualcosa di strano e leggermente inquietante a una sensazione di calma e luminosità.

Los espejos situados sobre los lavamanos no son superficies reflectantes ordinarias, sino pantallas LCD que proyectan imágenes de los usuarios del lavabo tomadas por cámaras ocultas. El efecto, extraño y ligeramente perturbador, contribuye, sin embargo, a transmitir una sensación de calma y luminosidad.

Les miroirs situés au-dessus des lavabos ne sont pas des surfaces réfléchissantes ordinaires, mais des écrans LCD qui projettent des images prises par des caméras cachées des utilisateurs du lavabo. L'effet, étrange et légèrement perturbateur, contribue sans aucun doute à transmettre une sensation de calme et de luminosité.

De spiegels boven de wastafels blijken LCD-schermen waarop beelden te zien zijn van de toiletbezoekers die zijn opgenomen met verborgen camera's. Het vervreemdende effect dat hierdoor ontstaat draagt echter wel bij aan een gevoel van rust en helderheid.

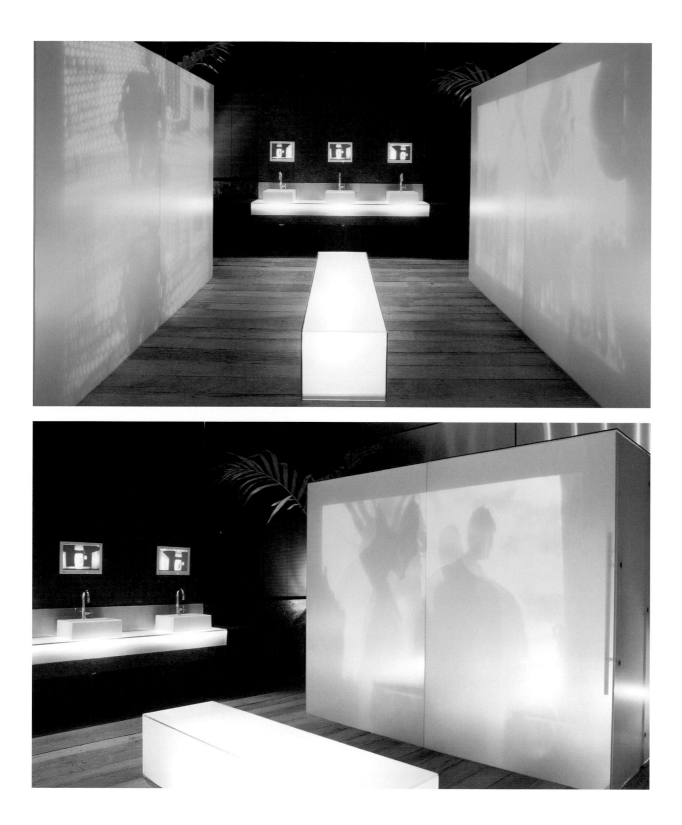

N°OCH

This bathroom was designed with the intention of avoiding any obvious historical and cultural references. The menu of this restaurant in the heart of the cosmopolitan city of New York is based on one of the stars of Asian cuisine – Chinese noodles – and their long, thin shape is subtly suggested in the design of the bathrooms, which display textures built up with sinuous lines and molded objects in wavy shapes.

Le linee di questo bagno si scostano nettamente da evidenti riferimenti storici e culturali. In mezzo alla città cosmopolita di New York, questo ristorante serve un menu basato su uno degli alimenti asiatici per eccellenza – i *noodles* –, e la loro forma sottile e allungata si insinua in maniera sofisticata nel disegno dei bagni, attraverso linee sinuose e oggetti modellati con contorni ondulati.

Este cuarto de baño se ha configurado con el fin de huir de referencias históricas y culturales evidentes. En el centro de la cosmopolita ciudad de Nueva York, se sirve un menú basado en uno de los alimentos asiáticos por excelencia: los fideos chinos; su forma delgada y alargada se insinúa sutilmente en el diseño de los baños, a través de una textura de líneas sinuosas y objetos de contornos ondulados.

Cette salle de bain a été imaginée sans s'appuyer sur des références historiques et culturelles trop évidentes. Dans le centre de la très cosmopolite ville de New York, on sert un menu basé sur un des aliments asiatiques les plus typiques – les vermicelles chinois –; cette forme fine et allongée est subtilement reprise dans le design des toilettes où des lignes sinueuses et des objets aux contours ondulés dessinent l'espace.

Deze plee heeft werkelijk lak aan alle bestaande historische en culturele toiletconventies. Midden in de kosmopolitische stad New York wordt een menu geserveerd gebaseerd op het ultieme Aziatische voedingsmiddel: mie. De slanke en lange vorm is op subtiele wijze terug te zien in de kronkelige lijnen en golvende contouren van dit ontwerp.

Architect: Karim Rashid Design
Year: 2004
Photography: Brian Park
Location: New York, USA

CAFÉ LE FRANCE

Color is an effective transmitter of emotions and feelings, and this bathroom bears witness to this fact with its two-color combination. The walls, painted an intense violet blue, bear three sumptuous gilt-framed mirrors, which are the sum total of the decoration and break up the uniformity of the color. A glass toilet introduces a touch of modernity into a space otherwise dominated by French baroque.

Il colore è un efficace veicolo di emozioni e sentimenti, così come dimostra questo bagno che gioca ad abbinare due diverse tonalità. Alle pareti, dipinte di un intenso blu-violetto, sono appesi tre sontuosi specchi dorati che costituiscono l'unico elemento di arredo e spezzano l'uniformità del colore. Un lavabo di vetro introduce un po' di modernità in uno spazio dominato dal barocco francese.

El color es un eficaz vehículo de emociones y sentimientos, y de ello da buena cuenta este baño que juega con la combinación de dos tonalidades. De las paredes, pintadas de un intenso azul violeta, cuelgan tres suntuosos espejos dorados que suponen la única decoración y rompen con la uniformidad del color. Un lavabo de cristal introduce modernidad en un espacio dominado por el barroquismo francés.

La couleur transmet efficacement les émotions et les sentiments ; ces toilettes en rendent compte en jouant et en combinant deux tonalités différentes. Sur les murs, peints d'un bleu violet intense, sont accrochés trois superbes miroirs dorés. Ils constituent la seule décoration et cassent l'uniformité de la couleur. Un lavabo en verre introduit une touche de modernité dans cet espace dominé par le style baroque français.

Kleur speelt een grote rol bij het overbrengen van emoties en gevoelens en daar is deze wc, waarbij gespeeld wordt met twee kleurschakeringen, een duidelijk voorbeeld van. De muren zijn geschilderd in een intens violetblauw en behangen met drie prachtige goudkleurige spiegels die de enige decoratie vormen en de kleureenheid verbreken. De glazen wastafel geeft een modern toefje aan deze barokke Franse ruimte.

Architect: Kristian Gavoille
Year: 2002
Photography: Kristian Gavoille
Location: Perpignan, France

VILLA BAKKE

Villa Bakke is a private residence which also serves as an exhibition space for art works. Two parallel nuclei, one made of concrete and the other of aluminum, make up the space where the public bathrooms are situated, designed for visitors to the exhibitions. An opaque glass wall separates, on one side, the guests' washbasin from the main bathroom, and, on the other, the washbasin from the stairs leading to the terrace.

Villa Bakke è una residenza privata che ospita anche mostre d'arte. Due nuclei paralleli, uno realizzato in calcestruzzo e l'altro in alluminio, formano lo spazio dove si trovano i bagni pubblici, a uso dei visitatori delle mostre. Da un lato, una parete di cristallo opaca separa il lavabo degli ospiti dal bagno principale e, dall'altro, separa il lavabo dalle scale che portano sulla terrazza.

Villa Bakke es una residencia privada que se utiliza también como espacio de exhibición de obras de arte. Dos núcleos paralelos, uno realizado en cemento y otro en aluminio, configuran el espacio donde se encuentra el baño público, pensado para los visitantes de las exposiciones. Una pared de cristal opaca separa, por un lado, el lavabo de invitados del baño principal, y por el otro, el lavabo de las escaleras que llevan a la terraza.

Villa Bakke est une résidence privée qui est également utilisée comme un espace d'exposition d'œuvres d'art. Deux noyaux parallèles, l'un en béton et l'autre en aluminium, structurent l'espace où se trouvent les toilettes publiques créées pour les visiteurs des expositions. Une paroi en verre opaque sépare d'un côté le lavabo des invités des toilettes principales, et de l'autre, le lavabo des escaliers qui mènent à la terrasse.

Villa Bakke is een privé-verblijf dat tevens wordt gebruikt als expositieruimte. De kunstliefhebbers kunnen hun behoefte doen in twee parallelle wc's, de ene gebouwd van aluminium en de andere van beton. De wastafels en toiletten zijn van elkaar gescheiden door een ondoorzichtige glazen wand.

Architect: MMW Studio34
Photography: Jiri Havran
Location: Oslo, Norway

FÒRUM DE LAS CULTURAS

Barcelona has once again expanded its urban infrastructure as a result of the celebration of the Fòrum de las Culturas in 2004, and it called on the services of well-known architects for this purpose. The various bathrooms on the grounds were designed to receive a large number of visitors. Here, the most arresting feature is the lighting, which floods the spaces with a brightly colored, uniform light.

In occasione della celebrazione del Fòrum de las Culturas nel 2004, Barcellona si è arricchita nuovamente di altre infrastrutture la cui realizzazione è stata opera di noti architetti. I diversi bagni sono stati disegnati per accogliere un gran numero di visitatori. Il loro punto di forza è l'illuminazione, che immerge lo spazio in una luce uniforme dalle tonalità intense.

Con motivo de la celebración del Fòrum de las Culturas en el 2004, Barcelona ha vuelto a engrosar su infraestructura urbana y ha contado para ello con la participación de conocidos arquitectos. Los diversos sanitarios del recinto están diseñados para acoger a un gran número de visitantes. El punto más importante es la iluminación, que sumerge el espacio en una luz uniforme de intensas tonalidades.

Dans le but de célébrer le Forum des Cultures de 2004, Barcelone a de nouveau enrichi son infrastructure urbaine en comptant pour cela sur la participation d'architectes connus. Les différents sanitaires de cet espace ont été conçus pour accueillir un grand nombre de visiteurs. L'éclairage constitue la réussite la plus surprenante ; elle envahit l'espace d'une lumière uniforme aux tonalités intenses.

Barcelona heeft het "Fòrum de las Culturas" in 2004 aangegrepen voor een opmerkelijke stadsuitbreiding waar veel bekende architecten aan hebben meegewerkt. De verschillende toiletunits van het complex zijn ontworpen om grote hoeveelheden mensen op te vangen. Het meest opvallende is de verlichting, die de ruimte onderdompelt in een uniform en intens licht.

Architect: Fòrum de las Culturas
Year: 2004
Photography: Joan Bonell
Location: Barcelona, Spain

CoCoon CLUB

Splashes of darkness swathe the interior of this bathroom in the form of anthracite-gray layers that cut across the walls and ceiling. This effect is complemented by the black terrazzo floor, the doors hidden behind a fractal image in cold colors that sets off the texture of the pine branches, and the cloudy mirrors (fitted with monitors) above each washbasin, an expression of the vital constants of all things without life.

Un'oscurità soffusa pervade l'interno di questo bagno dove strati grigi di antracite solcano le pareti e il soffitto; un pavimento alla veneziana nero, delle porte nascoste dietro un'immagine frattale dai colori freddi che rimanda alla testura dei rami di pino, e degli specchi scuri dove sono stati incassati alcuni monitor, sopra ogni lavabo, sono l'espressione delle costanti vitali di tutte le cose prive di vita.

Soplos de oscuridad envuelven el interior de este baño con capas grises de antracita que surcan las paredes y el techo; un suelo negro de terrazo, unas puertas escondidas tras una imagen fractal de colores fríos que remite a la textura de las ramas de pino y unos espejos turbios sobre cada lavamanos, donde se han encajado unos monitores, expresan las constantes vitales de todas las cosas sin vida.

Des souffles d'obscurité envahissent l'intérieur de ces toilettes ; c'est l'effet produit par les couches gris anthracite qui sillonnent les murs et le plafond ; un sol en granit noir, des portes cachées par une image fractale aux couleurs froides qui rappelle la structure des branches de pin, et des miroirs troubles où l'on a encastré des écrans au-dessus de chaque lavabo, expression des constantes vitales de toutes les choses sans vie.

Zuchtjes duisternis omhullen dit toilet met grijze laagjes antraciet die de wanden en het plafond doorklieven. De vloer is van zwart plavuis en de deuren gaan schuil achter een beeld in koele kleuren dat doet denken aan de takken van een pijnboom. In de troebele spiegels boven de fonteintjes zijn monitoren gemonteerd als uiting van de levensfunctie van alle levensloze objecten.

Architect: 3deluxe
Year: 2004
Photography: Emanuel Raab
Location: Frankfurt, Germany

CLAN CAFFÈ

The interior of the Clan Caffè, situated in a historic palace, is characterized by a versatility whose greatest virtue is the mixture of materials. The bathrooms play their part, with their combination of neutral colors and splashes of pink and blue which, along with the white flowers dotting the surface of the mirrors and the back-lit walls, immerse the space in a pop-art atmosphere full of vitality and sparkle.

Il Clan Caffè, situato in un antico palazzo storico, svela degli interni variegati la cui maggior virtù è la mescolanza di materiali diversi, caratteristica che distingue anche il bagno. Qui una combinazione di colori neutri e spruzzi blu e rosa, il bianco dei fiori sparsi sulla superficie e la retroilluminazione delle pareti, immergono lo spazio in un ambiente pop pieno di vitalità e freschezza.

Situado en un antiguo palacio histórico, el Clan Caffè revela un interior polifacético que hace de la mezcla de materiales su mayor virtud. De ello participan también los baños con una combinación de colores neutros y salpicaduras azules y rosas que, sumada a las flores blancas que adornan la superficie de los espejos y a la retroiluminación de las paredes, sumergen el espacio en un ambiente pop lleno de vitalidad y frescura.

Situé dans un ancien palais historique, le Clan Caffè dévoile un intérieur à facettes multiples grâce au mélange ingénieux des matériaux. On n'y a pas négligé les toilettes ; une combinaison de couleurs neutres et de tâches bleues et roses auxquelles il faut ajouter les fleurs blanches qui ornent la surface des miroirs et la réflexion de la lumière sur les murs, inondent l'espace pour créer une atmosphère pop pleine de vitalité et de fraîcheur.

Het in een historisch paleis gevestigde Clan Caffè heeft een zeer veelzijdig interieur waarin op magistrale wijze verschillende materialen worden gecombineerd. Onderdeel daarvan is deze toiletruimte, waar neutrale tinten contrasteren met spetterende blauwe en roze kleuren die dit vertrek, samen met de witte bloemen op de spiegels en de retroverlichting aan de wanden, veranderen in een hip, levendig en fris geheel.

Architect: Maurizio Lai
Photography: Andrea Martiradonna
Location: Milan, Italy

The gray walls inside the cubicle contrast with the antechamber, where white is the predominant color on the walls and floors.

Le pareti grigie dell'interno del WC contrastano con l'anticamera, dove il bianco è il colore predominante, presente sulle pareti e sul pavimento.

Las paredes grises del interior del váter contrastan con la antesala, donde el blanco es el color predominante presente en las paredes y los suelos.

Les murs gris de l'intérieur des W.C. tranchent avec le blanc de l'antichambre, couleur qui prédomine sur les murs et le sol.

De grijze wanden van de kleinste kamertjes zijn weer compleet anders dan het voorportaal, waar wit de overheersende kleur is in de wanden en de vloer.

RAIN

A large circular doorway leads to the anteroom of this bar's bathroom, a lounge with illuminated cubic tables and suspended circular Plexiglass seats. Designed to alleviate the wait for an occupied cubicle, or simply to operate as a space for interaction, it is a prelude to what comes next, in the bathroom itself.

Attraverso un grande portico circolare si accede all'anticamera dei servizi di questo bar, una sala che comprende sedie circolari in plexiglas così come tavoli cubici illuminati. Destinato a rendere più amena l'attesa nel caso in cui il WC sia occupato, o semplicemente a favorire l'interazione, questo spazio è un preludio a ciò che accadrà di seguito, nei bagni propriamente detti.

A través de una gran abertura circular se accede a la antesala de los excusados de este bar, que incorpora asientos suspendidos engastados en semiesferas de plexiglás y mesas cúbicas iluminadas. Destinado a hacer más amena la espera ante la eventualidad de que el váter esté ocupado o, simplemente, a funcionar como ámbito de interacción, este lounge es un preludio de lo que acontece a continuación, en los lavabos propiamente dichos.

On accède à l'antichambre de ce bar en passant par un grand portail circulaire et par un lounge meublé avec des sièges circulaires en plexiglas suspendus au plafond et des tables cubiques éclairées. Destinée à rendre l'attente plus agréable lorsque les W.C. sont occupés ou tout simplement à servir de lieu d'interaction, c'est un prélude de ce qui arrive ensuite, dans les toilettes proprement dites.

Via een grote, cirkelvormige vestibule kom je in het voorvertrek van de wc's van deze bar, een lounge met ronde zitmeubelen van hangend plexiglas en verlichte kubustafels. Dit verblijf, dat een eventueel oponthoud vanwege een bezet toilet moet veraangenamen en tevens dienstdoet als interactieruimte, is een voorbode van hetgeen zich aangrenzend bevindt, namelijk de wc's zelf.

Architect: II by IV Design Associates
Year: 2001
Photography: David Whittaker
Location: Toronto, Canada

METEORIT

The distinctive feature of this bathroom is the fact that it directs the visitor to the outside world by taking advantage of the vaulted roof, which makes it possible to capture sunlight to the maximum. The most difficult aspects were the geometric control and the use of wood on the curved surfaces. The mirror below is fitted with several light sources to complement the interior lighting. In the washbasin area, the surface serves several purposes, such as a trash can and a dispenser of paper towels.

La peculiarità di questo bagno risiede nel suo rivolgersi all'esterno ottenuta mediante il soffitto a volta che permette di catturare il massimo di luce naturale. Tra le principali difficoltà del progetto, il controllo geometrico e l'uso del legno nelle superfici curve. Sotto, lo specchio dispone di diversi punti luce che completano l'illuminazione interna. Nella zona del lavabo, è stata realizzata una superficie polifunzionale che comprende un contenitore e un dispenser di salviettine di carta.

La peculiaridad de este baño reside en su orientación hacia el exterior, que se obtiene con una cubierta abovedada que permite captar el máximo de luz natural. Uno de los aspectos que supuso mayor dificultad fue el control de las geometrías y el uso de la madera en las superficies curvas. Más abajo, los espejos disponen de diferentes puntos de luz para complementar la iluminación interior. En la zona de los lavamanos, se ha utilizado una superficie polifuncional que alberga un contenedor y un dispensador de toallitas de papel.

La particularité de ces toilettes réside dans son orientation vers l'extérieur grâce au plafond voûté qui permet de capter le maximum de lumière naturelle. Un des aspects les plus difficiles a été le respect des formes et l'utilisation du bois sur les surfaces courbes. En bas, le miroir dispose de différents points de lumière pour compléter l'éclairage intérieur. Dans la zone du lavabo, une surface à double usage a été utilisée: un container et un distributeur de serviettes en papier.

Het bijzondere van dit toilet is dat het naar buiten gericht is waardoor er zo veel mogelijk natuurlijk licht naar binnen kan stromen. Een van de moeilijkheden was de geometrische controle en het houtgebruik in het gewelfde dak. De spiegel bevat verschillende lichtpuntjes om de verlichting nog te versterken. Bij de wastafel is een polifunctioneel oppervlak aangebracht waarin een prullenbak en handdoekjesautomaat zitten.

Architect: Propeller Z
Year: 1998
Photography: Margherita Spiluttini
Location: Essen, Germany

CAMPUS CENTER IN ILLINOIS

This building on the campus of the Illinois Institute of Technology was designed to organize the dense network of pathways connecting the different parts of the campus. The bathrooms were drawn up on the basis of a triangle, with the urinals and the washbasins spread along two sides and the central space left open to facilitate circulation.

Questo edificio del campus dell'Istituto di Tecnologia dell'Illinois è stato realizzato con l'intenzione di strutturare meglio il denso reticolo di strade che mettono in comunicazione le diverse parti del campus. I bagni dell'edificio sono concepiti a partire da una struttura triangolare, con gli orinatoi e i lavabi disposti lungo i vertici e lo spazio centrale libero per una migliore circolazione.

Este edificio, situado en el campus del Instituto de Tecnología de Illinois, se realizó con la intención de organizar el denso entramado de vías que comunicaban las diferentes partes del campus. Los baños del edificio tiene la forma de un triángulo isósceles donde los urinarios y los lavamanos están dispuestos a lo largo de los dos lados iguales, para dejar el espacio central libre y garantizar una mejor circulación.

Ce bâtiment dans le campus de l'Institut de Technologie de l'Illinois a été conçu pour organiser le nœud dense des voies qui reliaient les différentes zones du campus. Les toilettes du bâtiment ont été imaginées en partant d'une structure triangulaire selon laquelle les urinoirs et les lavabos sont disposés tout le long de ses deux sommets, laissant l'espace central libre afin d'améliorer la circulation.

Dit gebouw op de campus van het Technologisch Instituut van Illinois is ontworpen met de bedoeling om de verschillende delen van de campus met elkaar te verbinden. De wc's van het gebouw bestaan uit een driehoekige structuur. De urinoirs en de wasruimtes zijn bereikbaar via twee hoeken terwijl de middenruimte is vrijgelaten om een betere doorgang te garanderen.

Architect: OMA
Year: 2003
Photography: Philippe Ruault
Location: Chicago, USA

M**A**NTRA

Going to the bathroom can become an adventure that holds in store surprises and chance encounters with unexpected objects. Confronting the North Pole in one corner, or watching bright snow slowly falling, form part of the dreamscape on offer to visitors to this bathroom. In the middle of the men's area, a stainless-steel cube incorporates a urinal and washbasin complete with ice.

Andare in bagno può diventare un vero e proprio viaggio disseminato di sorprese e incontri casuali con oggetti impensabili. Come se si trattasse di un sogno, entrando in questo bagno ci si può avvicinare al Polo Nord in un angolo della stanza, o si può osservare come la neve cada lenta e luminosa. In mezzo alla zona maschile, un cubo di acciaio inossidabile ingloba un orinatoio e un lavabo pieni di ghiaccio.

Ir al cuarto de baño puede convertirse en todo un viaje que nos depara sorpresas y encuentros casuales con objetos insospechados. Aproximarse al polo Norte en un rincón del lavabo o ver caer lentamente unos copos luminescentes de nieve forma parte del sueño que se nos presenta al entrar aquí. En el centro de la zona masculina, un cubo de acero inoxidable incorpora un urinario y un lavamanos repletos de hielo.

Aller aux toilettes devient un vrai voyage dans lequel on peut vivre des surprises et tomber sur des objets inattendus. S'approcher du pôle Nord dans un recoin des lavabos ou voir tomber lentement la neige sont les décors proposés et destinés à nous faire rêver lorsqu'on entre ici. Au milieu de la partie réservée aux hommes, un cube d'acier inoxydable intègre un urinoir et un lavabo plein de glace.

Naar de wc gaan kan een hele ontdekkingsreis worden waarbij we oog in oog kunnen komen te staan met grote verrassingen. In een hoek van deze droomwereld kun je de Noordpool naderen en komt het licht van de sneeuw jc tegemoet. Midden in het herengedeelte staat een kubus van roestvrij staal waar een met ijs gevuld urinoir en een wasbak in zijn vormgegeven.

Architect: Office dA
Photography: John Horner
Location: Boston, USA

The body of this bathroom seems to be posing a thought-provoking question focusing on privacy, with its exterior mirrored walls reflecting the customers in the restaurant, who are unaware of being observed from the interior.

Privacy o voyeurismo? Una questione da risolvere tra le pareti di questo bagno, i cui specchi esterni riflettono le immagini dei clienti del ristorante, osservati ignari dall'interno.

Una cuestión aparece formulada en el cuerpo de este lavabo, una cuestión vertiginosa que se plantea la privacidad entre unas paredes que muestran un exterior de espejos donde se reflejan los clientes del restaurante, observados desde el interior sin que se aperciban de nuestra mirada.

Des questions viennent à l'esprit de celui qui utilise ces toilettes, des questions bizarres et surprenantes, lorsqu'il se trouve dans l'intimité où des miroirs externes reflètent les clients du restaurant. Il peut donc les observer depuis l'intérieur sans qu'ils se rendent compte de son regard.

De ontwerpers van deze ruimte spelen met de privacygevoelens van de bezoekers, want vanuit de wc-gedeeltes kun je via spiegels zien hoe anderen zich voor de spiegel optutten terwijl zij jou niet kunnen zien.

O² FITNESS CENTER

In recent years, a less aggressive image of the gym has emerged, and this has been made manifest in a more human design. In the O2 gym, the changing room area is a minimalist setting that induces calm and tranquillity and enhances concentration. This project is characterized by its gentle expansiveness, which represents a response to the concept of wellness and a holistic approach to lifestyle.

Negli ultimi anni si è imposto un tipo di ginnastica meno aggressiva, che ha influenzato il design delle relative infrastrutture. Nella palestra O2, la zona degli spogliatoi si presenta come un ambiente minimalista, traboccante di calma e tranquillità, ideale per la concentrazione. Il senso di ampiezza e delicatezza che caratterizza questo progetto rappresenta una risposta al concetto di benessere e un approccio olistico alla vita.

En los últimos años se ha ido imponiendo un tipo de gimnasio menos agresivo, que se traduce en un diseño más humano. En el gimnasio O2, la zona de vestuarios se presenta como un ambiente minimalista, rebosante de quietud y de calma que favorece el recogimiento. La amplitud y la suavidad caracterizan este proyecto, que ha surgido como respuesta al concepto de bienestar, un enfoque integral de este estilo de vida.

Au cours des dernières années, un style de gymnase moins agressif s'est imposé. Dans le gymnase O2, la partie des vestiaires revêt un caractère minimaliste, rempli de calme et de quiétude, ce qui favorise la concentration. L'espace et la douceur sont les mots qui qualifient ce projet, où le bien-être, axé sur une mise au point complète du style de vie, constitue le concept de base.

In de afgelopen jaren zijn er minder agressieve sportscholen ontwikkeld, hetgeen zich vertaalt in een menselijker ontwerp. In de sportschool O2 is het kleedkamergedeelte een minimalistisch vertrek, waar rust en kalmte heersen die bijdragen aan de ingetogenheid.

Architect: Alonso Balaguer
Photography: Josep M. Molinos
Location: Barcelona, Spain

This project is guided by a Zen esthetic that encourages introspection.

Questo progetto si caratterizza per la sua estetica Zen che favorisce l'introspezione.

El proyecto está regido por una estética Zen que favorece la introspección interior.

Le projet est régi par une esthétique zen qui favorise la recherche introspective.

Dit project wordt gekenmerkt door ruimte en zachtheid als antwoord op een zen-concept waarbij lichaam en geest één zijn en niet onafhankelijk van elkaar kunnen worden ontwikkeld.

HARVEY NICHOLS RESTAURANT

Reflections turn a visit to this bathroom into a journey through a tunnel of light and color, which seems to stretch to infinity as a result of the mirrored façade that covers the entire back wall. Above the washbasins, a host of small circular mirrors reflect the green surface in front of it and merge with other circles in the form of white spotlights that emphasize the futuristic look.

I riflessi trasformano la visita a questo bagno in un viaggio attraverso un tunnel di luci e di colori, che sembra estendersi all'infinito grazie alla facciata a vetrata che riveste l'intera parete posteriore. Sui lavabi, un'infinità di piccoli specchi circolari riflette l'antistante superficie verde, mentre altri cerchi incassati non sono altro che faretti a luce bianca che mettono in risalto l'ambiente futurista.

Los reflejos convierten la visita a este excusado en un viaje por un túnel de luz y de color. Éste parece extenderse hasta el infinito gracias a la fachada de espejo que recubre toda la pared posterior. Sobre los lavamanos, una infinidad de pequeños espejos circulares refleja la superficie verde que tienen delante, mientras que otros círculos intercalados son focos de luz blanca que exaltan el ambiente futurista.

Les reflets permettent à celui qui utilise ces toilettes de faire un voyage en passant par un tunnel de lumière et de couleur qui semble s'étendre jusqu'à l'infini grâce aux panneaux de verre qui recouvrent tout le mur postérieur. Au-dessus des lavabos, une infinité de petits miroirs circulaires reflète la surface verte qu'ils ont en face, tandis que d'autres cercles intercalés sont des foyers de lumière blanche d'où émane une atmosphère futuriste.

Door de reflectie is het bezoek aan dit toilet als een reis door een tunnel van licht. Die reis lijkt eindeloos vanwege de spiegel die aan de achterwand is gemonteerd. Boven de wastafels weerkaatsen kleine ronde spiegels het groene oppervlak ervoor terwijl andere kleine cirkelvormen spotjes blijken te zijn die wit licht verspreiden, wat het futuristische effect verder versterkt.

Architect: Lifschutz Davidson
Photography: Chris Gascoigne/View
Location: Manchester, UK

DAYCARE IN PAMPLONA

Architecture is clear, elemental and perfect when it expresses a culture's values. The carefully thought out design of this daycare perhaps reflects Terragni's intention when he built a playschool in Como. The bathroom has been drawn up as an unpretentious space, somewhere between structure and space, that is flooded with light.

L'architettura nasce nitida, elementare e perfetta quando è l'espressione di un popolo che seleziona, osserva ed apprezza i risultati che, diligentemente rielaborati, esprimono i loro valori… Nel corpo "rielaborato" di questo asilo infantile, risuonano forse le parole del noto architetto Giuseppe Terragni a proposito dell'Asilo Sant'Elia realizzato a Como. Il bagno è concepito come uno spazio luminoso, privo di giochetti intellettuali tra struttura e volume.

La arquitectura surge límpida, elemental y perfecta cuando es la expresión de un pueblo que selecciona, observa y aprecia los resultados que diligentemente reelaborados, expresan sus valores… En el cuerpo "reelaborado" de esta guardería resuenan, tal vez, las palabras de Terragni a propósito del parvulario que construyó en Como. El baño se proyecta como un espacio luminoso y sin intelectualismos entre estructura y volumen.

L'architecture est limpide, élémentaire et parfaite quand elle devient l'expression d'un peuple qui choisit, observe et apprécie les résultats qui diligemment réélaborés, expriment leurs valeurs… Dans le corps "réélaboré" de cette garderie d'enfants, les mots de Terragni résonnent peut-être encore dans le jardin d'enfants qu'il a construit à Côme. Les toilettes y ont été pensées comme un espace lumineux et sans intellectualisme entre structure et volume.

De architectuur is zuiver, elementair en perfect als het de expressie is van een gemeenschap die zoekt naar ontwerpen die, als ze zorgvuldig worden aangepast, hun waarden weergeven. Het "aangepaste" hoofdonderkomen van deze crèche doet in alles denken aan de kleuterschool die Terragni in Como heeft gebouwd.

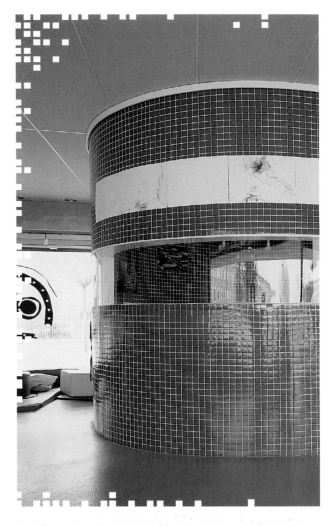

Architect: Capilla Vallejo Arquitectos
Year: 2000
Photography: José Manuel Cutillas
Location: Pamplona, Spain

A circular structure in the center of the classroom contains the bath-rooms. The interior is generously decorated in bright blue, reflecting the needs of its users.

Una struttura circolare situata al centro dell'aula ospita i bagni, i cui interni, abbondantemente decorati e realizzati in un azzurro vivo, ri-flettono le esigenze dei loro utenti.

Una estructura circular situada en el centro de la clase da cabida a los baños, cuyo interior, abundantemente decorado y realizado en un azul vivo, refleja las necesidades de sus usuarios.

Dans une structure circulaire située au centre de la classe se trou-vent les toilettes. L'intérieur, richement décoré et peint en bleu vif, re-flète l'état d'esprit de ses utilisateurs.

De wc is een lichte, cirkelvormige ruimte in het midden van de klas. Het interieur is weelderig gedecoreerd en gerealiseerd in een leven-dige blauwe kleur, overeenkomstig de voorkeuren van de gebruikers.

VI^LLAGE CINEMAS INTERNATIONAL

The curved walls and sloping roof of the bathrooms in this cinema create a sculptural space replete with theatricality, while additional dividing walls separate the various areas inside the bathroom. Simple but effective finishings, such as ceramics, metal and granite, have been combined with touches of bright red and blue mosaic to create a visually stimulating and attractive interior.

Le pareti curve e il soffitto inclinato dei bagni di questo cinema danno luogo a uno spazio scultoreo e pieno di teatralità; i diversi ambienti sono separati mediante pareti divisorie aggiuntive. Finiture semplici ma efficaci, come la ceramica, il metallo e il granito, sono state abbinate a dettagli di mosaico in toni azzurro e rosso brillante, che creano degli interni stimolanti e attraenti dal punto di vista visivo.

Las paredes curvadas y el techo inclinado de los sanitarios de este cine dan lugar a un espacio escultural y lleno de teatralidad, mientras que otras paredes divisorias adicionales separan los diversos ámbitos dentro del baño. Acabados sencillos, aunque efectivos, como la cerámica, el metal y el granito, se han combinado con toques de mosaicos azules y rojos brillantes que crean un interior visualmente estimulante y atractivo.

Les murs courbes et le plafond incliné des sanitaires de ce cinéma donnent lieu à un espace sculptural, rempli de théâtralité. D'autres parois créent à l'intérieur des toilettes des séparations supplémentaires qui offrent des ambiances différentes. Des finitions simples mais efficaces comme la céramique, le métal et le granit ont été combinées avec des touches de mosaïques bleue et rouge brillant créant ainsi un intérieur stimulant et attrayant.

De gebogen muren en het kantelende dak van het sanitair van deze bioscoop omhullen een prachtige, theatrale ruimte, terwijl andere scheidingswanden de verschillende compartimenten van de wc's van elkaar afscheiden. De eenvoudige en effectieve afwerking, waarbij keramiek, metaal en graniet worden gecombineerd met glinsterende blauwe en rode mozaïeken, draagt bij aan een visueel aantrekkelijk en stimulerend interieur.

Architect: Jestico + Whiles
Year: 2002
Photography: Ales Jungmann
Location: Prague, Czech Republic

An elliptical unit situated in the center of the men's area contains the washbasins, but it leaves sufficient space for fluid circulation.

Un'unità ellittica situata al centro del bagno degli uomini ingloba i lavamani, lasciando quindi spazio sufficiente per una circolazione fluida.

Una unidad elíptica situada en el centro del baño de hombres incorpora los lavamanos, de manera que haya espacio suficiente para una circulación fluida.

Une unité elliptique située au centre des toilettes pour homme intègre des lavabos laissant ainsi suffisamment d'espace pour circuler avec fluidité.

In een elliptische eenheid in het centrum van het herentoilet bevinden zich de wastafels, die zodanig zijn geplaatst dat er voldoende ruimte overblijft voor een goede doorstroming.

TA M AND GANG RESTAURANT

Eating can go beyond the mere alleviation of hunger and has always been associated with ritual and sensuality; all this is perfectly reflected in this restaurant's bathroom. The theatricality implicit in any ritual is manifested through the colors, materials, textures and forms that make up a setting reminiscent of a cubist painting, in which the straight line is the undisputed protagonist.

Da sempre il consumo di alimenti, al di là del mero appagamento della fame, comporta associazioni rituali e sensuali, come dimostra chiaramente il bagno di questo ristorante. La teatralità insita in qualsiasi rito si manifesta mediante colori, materiali, trame e forme che danno vita a uno scenario simile a un quadro cubista, dove la linea retta è la protagonista indiscutibile.

El consumo de alimentos, más allá de la mera satisfacción del hambre, trae consigo desde siempre asociaciones rituales y sensuales, y de ello da buena cuenta el baño de este restaurante. La teatralidad que implica cualquier rito se manifiesta en este lavabo a través de colores, materiales, texturas y formas, que configuran un escenario parecido a un cuadro cubista.

La consommation d'aliments, au-delà de satisfaire purement la faim, est associée depuis toujours à des rituels et des sensations ; les toilettes de ce restaurant n'y sont pas laissées pour compte. La théâtralité qu'implique tout rite se manifeste dans ces toilettes à travers des couleurs, des matériaux, des textures et des formes qui ressemblent au scénario d'un tableau cubiste dans lequel la ligne droite est indiscutablement l'élément principal.

Voedselconsumptie dient niet enkel om honger te stillen, maar heeft ook altijd een rituele en sensuele component, aldus de filosofie van dit restaurant. Dat blijkt duidelijk uit dit wc-ontwerp. Het theatrale dat ten grondslag ligt aan iedere rite uit zich in dit toilet in het gebruik van de kleuren, materialen en vormen die samen een decor scheppen vergelijkbaar met een kubistisch schilderij, waarin de rechte lijn de onbetwiste hoofdrol opeist.

Architect: Satmoko Ball Architecture Design
Photography: Sue Barr/View
Location: London, UK

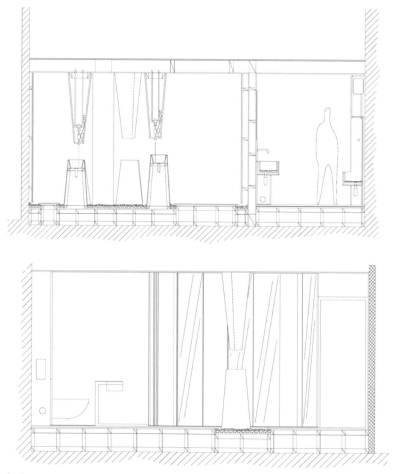

Section

Straight lines mold objects in which metal and stone merge together, where water mingles with light and an array of reflections endow the space with an aura of purity.

La linea retta modella oggetti dove si confondono il metallo e la pietra, dove l'acqua si mescola con la luce e molteplici riflessi avvolgono lo spazio in un'aura di purezza.

La línea recta moldea objetos en que el metal y la piedra se confunden, el agua se mezcla con la luz y múltiples reflejos envuelven el espacio en un aura de pureza.

La ligne droite façonne des objets dans lesquels le métal et la pierre se confondent, l'eau se mélange à la lumière et de multiples reflets enveloppent l'espace dans une aura de pureté.

De rechte lijn vervormt objecten waarin metaal en steen versmelten, water zich mengt met licht en de vele reflecties de ruimte omhullen in een aura van puurheid.

RESIDENTIAL BATHROOMS

Clinics, hospitals and residences are places not generally associated with esthetic revolutions. However, the projects detailed below stand out for their effective expression of well-being and tranquility because of an informal design approach. Hotels, in contrast, tend to treat bathrooms as a theatrical stage and often come up with very imaginative ideas. In both cases, these are bathrooms which a resident will usually use more than once, as they belong to buildings designed for relatively long stays.

In genere le cliniche, gli ospedali e gli alberghi sono spazi che si prestano poco alla rivoluzione estetica. Ciò nonostante, i progetti esposti qui di seguito si fanno notare per l'efficacia con cui riescono a trasmettere sensazioni di benessere e tranquillità mediante un design tutt'altro che trascurato. Negli alberghi, al contrario, si tende a trattare il bagno come uno scenario teatrale, adottando soluzioni davvero fantasiose. In entrambi i casi, si tratta di servizi igienici che il cliente possibilmente utilizzerà più di una volta, visto che si tratta di spazi pensati per un soggiorno relativamente lungo.

Clínicas, hospitales y residencias son espacios por lo general poco dados a la revolución visual. Sin embargo, los proyectos expuestos a continuación destacan por una eficaz transmisión de sensaciones de bienestar y tranquilidad mediante un diseño de manera descuidada. Los hoteles, por el contrario, tienden a tratar el baño como un escenario teatral, y suelen aportar soluciones muy imaginativas. En ambos casos, se trata de aseos que el cliente supuestamente utilizará más de una vez, pues son espacios pensados para una estancia relativamente duradera.

Les cliniques, les hôpitaux et les résidences sont des espaces en général peu enclins à une révolution visuelle. Cependant, les projets exposés à la suite se distinguent des autres car ils transmettent des sensations de bien-être et de tranquillité grâce à un design que l'on pourrait croire « négligé ». Les hôtels, au contraire, tendent à traiter les toilettes comme une scène théâtrale et apportent souvent des solutions très imaginatives. Dans les deux cas, ce sont des toilettes que le client utilisera bien évidemment plus d'une fois puisqu'il s'agit d'espaces pensés pour un séjour relativement long.

Klinieken en ziekenhuizen zijn nu niet bij uitstek plekken voor revolutionair design. De voorbeelden die hier onder volgen onderscheiden zich echter vanwege de efficiënte wijze waarop het wc-ontwerp bijdraagt aan een gevoel van rust en welbehagen. Hotels bekijken de toiletruimte daarentegen veel theatraler en komen vaak met zeer fantasierijke oplossingen. In beide gevallen gaat het om wc's die waarschijnlijk vaker worden gebruikt door de klanten en zijn ingericht voor een langer verblijf.

HOTEL SIDE

This project is part of the Hotel Side in Hamburg, created by Matteo Thun along with the theater director Robert Wilson and the architects Alsop and Stoermer. In the middle of an oasis in which sensory reactions are heightened by the lighting, and the space is reduced to the beauty of economy and simplicity, this public bathroom seems to have been borrowed from a stage set for an evocative and imaginative theater piece.

Il presente progetto appartiene all'Hotel Side di Amburgo, realizzato da Matteo Thun insieme allo scenografo Robert Wilson e agli architetti Alsop e Stoermer. In mezzo a un'oasi dove i sensi prendono forma grazie alla luce, e lo spazio viene trattato con economia e semplicità, si trova questo bagno pubblico che sembra sbucare dallo scenario di un'opera drammatica, toccante e fantasiosa.

El presente proyecto pertenece al Hotel Side de Hamburgo, realizado por Matteo Thun junto al escenógrafo Robert Wilson y a los arquitectos Alsop y Stoermer. En medio de un oasis donde los sentidos se hacen corpóreos gracias a la luz, y el espacio es reducido a la belleza de la economía y la simplicidad, se presenta este cuarto de baño público que parece sacado del escenario de una obra dramática sugerente e imaginativa.

Le projet présenté appartient à l'Hotel Side de Hambourg ; il a été réalisé par Matteo Thun en collaboration avec le metteur en scène Robert Wilson et les architectes Alsop et Stoermer. Au milieu d'une oasis où les sens se font corporels grâce à la lumière et où l'espace se réduit à une beauté épurée et simple, on présente ces toilettes publiques qui semblent tout droit sorties d'un scénario d'une œuvre dramatique suggestive et imaginative.

Dit project bevindt zich in Hotel Side in Hamburg en is uitgevoerd door Matteo Thun, decorontwerper Robert Wilson en de architecten Alsop en Stoermer. Te midden van een oase waar de ruimte beperkt is gebleven tot de schoonheid van efficiëntie en eenvoud, bevindt zich dit openbare toilet dat zo uit van het podium van een toneelstuk lijkt te komen.

Architect: Matteo Thun
Photography: c/o idpa
Location: Hamburg, Germany

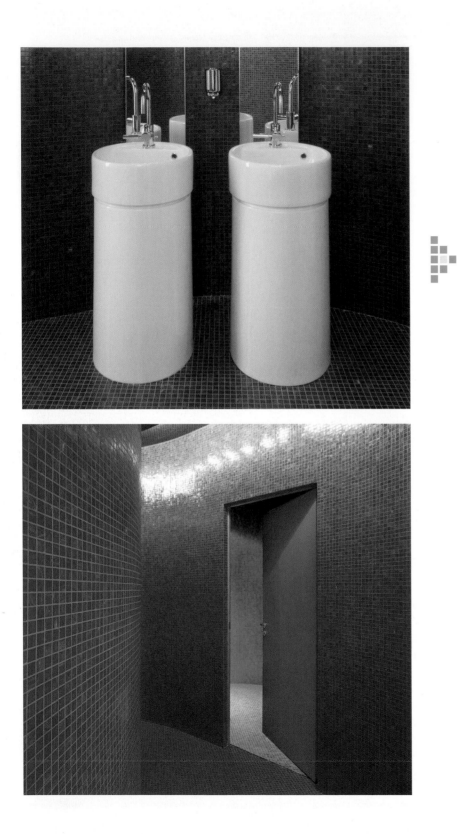

The lyricism of the lighting, the softness of the colors and the sinuousity of the concentric forms, which seem to embrace infinity, totality and timelessness, raise a setting often marked by tawdriness to a sphere of elegance and beauty that takes on all the complexity of simplicity.

Il lirismo della luce, la morbidezza dei colori, la sinuosità delle forme concentriche che abbracciano l'infinito, la totalità e l'atemporalità, elevano uno spazio spesso ritenuto di cattivo gusto a una sfera di eleganza e bellezza velata da un'apparente semplicità.

El lirismo de la luz, la suavidad de los colores y la sinuosidad de las formas concéntricas que abrazan el infinito, la totalidad y la intemporalidad, elevan un espacio a menudo vulgar a una esfera de elegancia y hermosura que abarca toda la complejidad de la sencillez.

Le lyrisme de la lumière, la douceur des couleurs et la sinuosité des formes concentriques qui embrassent l'infini, la totalité et l'intemporalité, élèvent un espace souvent vulgaire à une sphère d'élégance et de beauté qui résume toute la complexité de la simplicité.

De lyriek van het licht, de zachte kleuren en kronkelige, concentrische vormen die het oneindige lijken te omarmen, de totaliteit en tijdloosheid tillen deze ruimte uit boven de dagelijkse werkelijkheid naar een sfeer van elegantie en pracht die tegelijkertijd uitmunt in eenvoud.

HOTEL ALEPH

The public bathrooms in this hotel (entirely designed by Adam Tihany) are an intelligent continuation of the heaven/hell duality that echoes throughout the interior of the building. The totally red Aleph bathroom creates a certain dramatic effect by tiling the walls with red mosaics interspersed with strips of black granite made by Bisazza.

I bagni pubblici di questo albergo, il cui design è stato interamente curato da Adam Tihany, sono un'intelligente continuazione della dualità cielo-inferno, il filo conduttore che caratterizza le varie aree interne dell'edificio. A farla da padrone nel bagno di questo prestigioso hotel romano, è il colore rosso. Rossi sono infatti i mosaici Bisazza, con inserti in granito nero, che rivestono le pareti e che conferiscono all'ambiente un certo tocco drammatico.

Los baños públicos de este hotel, enteramente diseñado por Adam Tihany, son una inteligente continuación de la dualidad cielo-infierno que se recrea en todo el interior del edificio. Completamente rojo, el baño del Aleph alcanza cierto efecto dramático a través del revestimiento de las paredes, con mosaicos rojos fabricados por Bisazza en los que se intercalan tiras de granito negro.

Les toilettes publiques de cet hôtel, entièrement designé par Adam Tihany, sont une suite intelligente au duel ciel-enfer qui a été recréé à l'intérieur de tout le bâtiment. Totalement rouges, les toilettes de l'Aleph atteignent un certain effet dramatique grâce au revêtement des murs, des mosaïques rouges fabriquées par Bisazza dans lesquelles on a intercalé des bandes de granit noir.

De openbare toiletten van dit hotel, dat in zijn geheel is ontworpen door Adam Tihany, zijn een intelligent vervolg op de dualiteit hemel-hel die aanwezig is in het gehele interieur van dit gebouw. Deze in rood uitgevoerde ruimte heeft een zeker dramatisch effect op de bezoekers met name door de wandbekleding met rood mozaïekwerk van Bisazza afgewisseld met stroken grijs graniet.

Architect: Adam Tihany
Photography: Alberto Ferrero
Location: Rome, Italy

The bathrooms in the spa are very different in appearance from those in the hall. Pale colors and soft lighting are used to evoke the sky, a space representing relaxation and tranquility.

I bagni del centro termale mostrano un aspetto molto diverso da quelli della hall. Mediante colori chiari e un'illuminazione leggera si intende rappresentare il cielo, uno spazio dove regnano la quiete e il relax.

Los baños del spa muestran una apariencia muy distinta a los del vestíbulo. Colores claros y una iluminación suave se utilizan con la voluntad de escenificar el cielo, espacio de quietud y de relajación.

Les toilettes du centre thermal sont très différentes de celles du hall. Des couleurs claires et un éclairage doux ont été employées dans le but de mettre en scène le ciel, espace de quiétude et de relaxation.

De toiletten van de spa zijn compleet anders vormgegeven dan die in de hal. Het heldere kleurgebruik en de zachte verlichting dragen hier bij aan de hemelse sfeer van rust en ontspanning.

PRᴱVENTICUM RADIOLOGY CLINIC

In contrast to the coldness often associated with bathrooms for public use, those in this clinic show a warm, snug image enhanced by a meticulous attention to detail. The use of luxurious materials such as wood, marble and ceramics gives a subtle color scheme which, apart from providing a relaxing effect, conveys security and serenity to the patient who is going to be examined.

Contrariamente alla freddezza che con frequenza viene associata ai bagni pubblici, i servizi di questa clinica sono pervasi da un'atmosfera calda e avvolgente che presta molta attenzione ai particolari. L'utilizzo di materiali ricchi come il legno, il marmo e la ceramica, origina un accurato accostamento cromatico che, oltre a trasmettere un effetto rilassante, infonde sicurezza e serenità al paziente in visita alla clinica.

Contrariamente a la imagen fría que con frecuencia se asocia a los baños de uso público, los servicios de esta clínica proyectan una imagen cálida y envolvente que presta un especial cuidado al detalle. El empleo de materiales ricos como la madera, el mármol y la cerámica origina una sutil combinación cromática que, además de surtir un efecto relajante, transmite seguridad y serenidad al paciente que va a visitarse.

Contrairement à l'image froide qui est fréquemment associée aux toilettes publiques, les W.C. de cette clinique transmettent une image chaude et envoûtante en prêtant un soin particulier aux détails. L'emploi de matériaux riches comme le bois, le marbre et la céramique crée une subtile combinaison chromatique qui, outre à transmettre un effet relaxant, communique un sentiment de sécurité et de sérénité au patient qui y accède.

In tegenstelling tot het kille beeld dat vaak bestaat van openbare toiletten in gezondheidscentra is het sanitair van deze kliniek juist warm en omhullend, waarbij er veel oog is voor detail. Het gebruik van hoogwaardige materialen zoals hout, marmer en keramiek, die op subtiele wijze worden gecombineerd, werkt rustgevend en biedt veiligheid en vertrouwen aan de bezoekende patiënten.

Architect: Ulla Blennemann
Photography: Jörg Hempel/Photodesign
Location: Essen, Germany

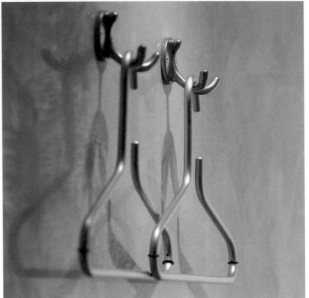

The significance of the small details makes this bathroom a space that is serene and attractive.

L'importanza dei piccoli dettagli fa di questo bagno uno spazio gradevole e sereno.

La relevancia de los pequeños detalles convierte este lavabo en un espacio sereno y agradable.

L'importance des petits détails transforme ces toilettes en un espace de tranquillité.

De relevantie van de kleine details versterken het rustgevende en aangename effect.

SANDERSON HOTEL

This theatrical, sensual, unconventional and detailed bathroom belongs to the Sanderson Hotel, a luxury city spa situated in the heart of London's West End. Philippe Starck has converted a building from the 1950s into an imaginary world that creates a dreamscape worthy of the fantasies of Cocteau, a surrealistic set of which the hotel's public toilet forms a fitting part.

Teatrale, sensuale, affatto convenzionale e curato nei minimi particolari. Così é il bagno del Sanderson Hotel, un elegante centro termale urbano situato nel cuore del West End londinese. Philippe Starck ha trasformato l'originale edificio degli anni '50 in un mondo immaginario che ricrea un universo da sogno degno delle fantasie di Cocteau: uno scenario surrealista in cui rientra anche il bagno pubblico dell'albergo.

Teatral, sensual, inconvencional y detallista es este baño perteneciente al Sanderson Hotel, un lujoso spa urbano situado en el corazón del West End londinense. Philippe Starck ha transformado un edificio de los años cincuenta en un mundo de imaginación que recrea un universo de ensoñación digno de las fantasías de Cocteau; un escenario surrealista del que forma parte el lavabo público del hotel.

Théâtral, sensuel, non conventionnel et détailliste sont les adjectifs qui servent à qualifier les toilettes du Sanderson Hotel, un luxueux centre thermal urbain situé dans le cœur du West End londonien. Philippe Starck a transformé un bâtiment des années cinquante en un monde d'imagination qui recrée un univers d'enchantement digne des fantaisies de Cocteau ; un scénario surréaliste dont les toilettes publiques de l'hôtel font partie.

Theatraal, sensueel, onconventioneel en gedetailleerd zijn de kenmerken van deze toiletruimte van het Sanderson Hotel, een luxueuze spa gesitueerd in het hart van het Londense West End. Philippe Starck heeft een gebouw uit de jaren vijftig omgetoverd tot een verbeeldingsvolle, surrealistische droomwereld, waar ook het toilet van het hotel deel van uitmaakt.

Architect: Philippe Starck
Year: 2000
Photography: Red Cover
Location: London, UK

 LE ROYAL MERIDIEN HOTEL

In the Royal Meridien Hotel in Hamburg, transparency and opacity represent two sides of a single coin: both facets are on show in the public bathrooms and work together to convey a sensation of luxury and modernity. One of the toilets is flooded with light and decorated in modern, pastel tones, while the other shows a more traditional look.

Semitrasparenza e opacità formano, nel Royal Meridien Hotel di Amburgo, le due facce di una stessa medaglia. Entrambe le qualità pervadono gli ambienti dei bagni pubblici al fine di trasmettere una sensazione di lusso e modernità. Uno dei bagni appare diafano, decorato in toni pastello e in stile moderno, mentre l'altro mette in luce un aspetto più tradizionale, con materiali nobili quali il legno e il marmo.

Translucidez y opacidad forman, en el Royal Meridien Hotel de Hamburgo, las dos caras de una misma moneda: ambas cualidades están representadas en los cuartos de baño públicos con el fin de transmitir la sensación de lujo y modernidad. Uno de los lavabos se muestra diáfano, decorado en tonos pastel, y moderno, mientras que el otro descubre su faceta más tradicional, con materiales nobles como la madera y el mármol.

Translucidité et opacité sont deux caractéristiques associées au design du Royal Meridien Hotel de Hambourg, tout comme les deux faces d'une même pièce de monnaie ; ces deux qualités sont représentées dans les toilettes publiques dans le but de transmettre une sensation de luxe et de modernité. Un des W.C. se montre diaphane et moderne, décoré dans des tons pastel, tandis que l'autre laisse découvrir un côté plus traditionnel, avec des matériaux nobles comme le bois et le marbre.

Transparantie en opaciteit vormen in het Royal Meridien Hotel in Hamburg twee kanten van dezelfde medaille. Beide kenmerken zijn ook vertegenwoordigd in de openbare closetruimtes van het hotel met als doel om de bezoekers een gevoel van luxe en moderniteit te geven. Een van de wc's is transparant uitgevoerd in moderne pastelkleuren, terwijl de andere traditioneler is met gebruik van mooie materialen als hout en marmer.

Architect: Feuring Hotelconsulting GmbH
Photography: Jörg Hempel/Photodesign
Location: Hamburg, Germany

The frontiers between traditional luxury and state-of-the-art design are blurred as the two merge together in this fascinating creation.

Il lusso tradizionale e il design più contemporaneo dissolvono i propri limiti per fondersi in questo interessante e armonico progetto.

El lujo tradicional y el diseño más contemporáneo disuelven sus fronteras para mezclarse en este interesante diseño.

Le luxe traditionnel et le design le plus contemporain s'interpénètrent et, en se mélangeant, créent un design intéressant et harmonieux.

Traditionele luxe en modern design ontmoeten elkaar in dit interessante ontwerp.

REHAB BASEL

This bathroom, set in a rehabilitation clinic, opts for innovative sensory experiences through the evocative use of acid green. The uniform color of the structure's finishing turns this bathroom into a distinctive, enclosed box. Elements such as the toilet, the washbasin and the white curtain, were incorporated like pieces of interior landscape, to break up the uniformity of the surrounding structure.

Questo bagno, all'interno di una clinica di riabilitazione, punta su nuove esperienze sensoriali mediante l'uso stimolante del colore verde acido. La finitura della struttura in un unico cromatismo trasforma questo bagno in una singolare scatola chiusa. Il WC, il lavabo e la tendina bianca non sono altro che elementi del paesaggio interno, inseriti per spezzare l'uniformità di tutto l'involucro.

Este baño, ubicado en una clínica de rehabilitación, apuesta por nuevas experiencias sensoriales mediante el uso sugerente del color verde ácido. El acabado de la estructura en un solo cromatismo lo convierte en una caja cerrada y singular. Los elementos como el inodoro, el lavamanos o la cortina blanca fueron incorporados como piezas del paisaje interior para romper la uniformidad de la estructura envolvente.

Ces toilettes, situées dans un centre de réhabilitation, misent sur de nouvelles expériences sensorielles en utilisant de manière suggestive le vert acidulé comme couleur. Les finitions de la structure d'un seul chromatisme transforment ces toilettes à la manière d'une singulière caisse fermée. Les W.C., le lavabo et le rideau blanc ont été incorporés comme des éléments du paysage intérieur afin de casser l'uniformité de la structure qui l'entoure.

Dit sanitair in een Zwitsers revalidatiecentrum probeert de zintuigen te prikkelen door het suggestieve gebruik van gifgroen. De afwerking in een enkele kleur verandert dit toilet in een gesloten doos. Elementen als de pot, de wasbak of het witte gordijn zijn in dit groene landschap ingepast om de uniformiteit van de omhullende structuur te doorbreken.

Architect: Herzog & De Meuron
Photography: Margherita Spiluttini
Location: Basel, Switzerland

HI HOTEL

The Hi Hotel breaks not only the codes of traditional luxury hotels but also the domestic rituals. It sets up an area of mobility and experimentation while allowing the user to feel autonomous and free to explore. This original washbasin, shared by both men and women, is not set inside the bathroom, as it is customary, but in the corridor in the hotel's reception area.

L'Hi Hotel rompe non solo tutti i canoni convenzionali del design alberghiero di lusso, ma anche i rituali domestici. L'albergo propone uno spazio di mobilità e al contempo di sperimentazione che consente all'utente di sentirsi autonomo e libero di esplorare. Questo originale lavabo, comune ai signori e alle signore, non si trova, come accade normalmente, all'interno del bagno, ma nello stesso corridoio occupato dalla zona della reception dell'hotel.

El Hi Hotel rompe no sólo con los códigos de la hotelería tradicional de lujo, sino también con los ritos domésticos. Propone un espacio de movilidad y de experimentación a la vez que permite al usuario sentirse autónomo y libre de explorar. Este original lavamanos, común para damas y caballeros, no se encuentra en el interior del baño, como es habitual, sino en el mismo pasillo de la zona de la recepción del hotel.

Le Hi Hotel rompt non seulement avec les codes de l'hôtellerie traditionnelle de luxe, mais aussi avec les rites domestiques. Il propose à la fois un espace de mobilité et d'expérimentation qui permet à l'utilisateur de se sentir autonome et libre d'explorer. Le lavabo très original, commun aux dames et aux hommes, ne se trouve pas, comme il en est coutume, à l'intérieur des toilettes, mais dans le couloir de la zone de réception de l'hôtel.

Het Hi Hotel breekt niet alleen met alle bestaande conventies van het traditionele luxe hotelwezen, maar ook met het gevoel van huiselijkheid. Het toilet is een ruimte vol beweging en experimenten waar de gebruiker op onderzoek kan uitgaan. De originele wastafel, die zowel voor dames als heren is, bevindt zich niet in een afgesloten ruimte, maar in het gangpad van de hotelreceptie.

Architect: Matali Crasset Productions
Photography: Christian Michel/View
Location: Nice, France

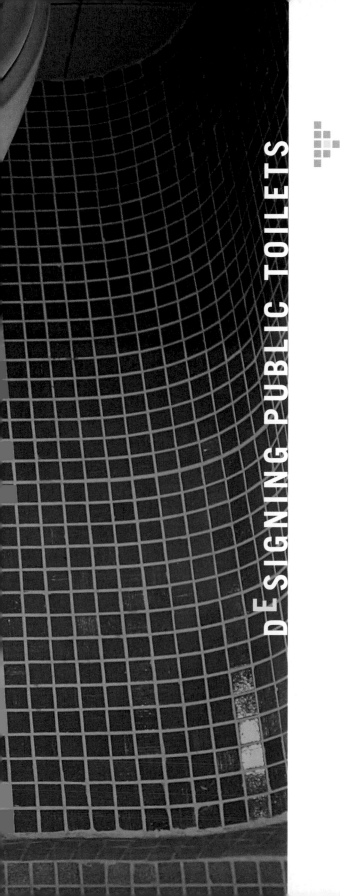

DESIGNING PUBLIC TOILETS

WORKING ENVIRONMENT

It is a proven fact that a well-structured bathroom fosters communication and improves the working environment, thereby also enhancing the performance of the labor force. At the same time, a bathroom can highlight a company's business values and provide information about its field of production. These factors are illustrated by the projects shown in this section – bathrooms attached to offices, stores, showrooms and shopping malls that present a functional and visually attractive design, especially adapted to the needs of the establishments in question.

È stato dimostrato che un bagno ben realizzato stimola la comunicazione e migliora l'ambiente di lavoro, facendo aumentare così il rendimento dei lavoratori. Allo stesso tempo, mette in rilievo i valori aziendali della società e apporta informazioni sul suo settore di produzione. I progetti che mostriamo di seguito in questa sezione ne sono un ottimo esempio: bagni appartenenti a studi e uffici, negozi, showroom e centri commerciali che presentano un design funzionale e visualmente attraente, appositamente adattato alle esigenze dei diversi gruppi di utenti.

Se ha comprobado que un baño bien estructurado fomenta la comunicación y mejora el ambiente laboral, lo que favorece el rendimiento del trabajador. Al mismo tiempo, pone de relieve los valores empresariales de la compañía y aporta información sobre el sector de producción de ésta. De ello dan buena cuenta los proyectos mostrados en este apartado, lavabos pertenecientes a oficinas, despachos, tiendas, showrooms y centros comerciales que presentan un diseño funcional y visualmente atractivo, especialmente adaptado a las necesidades de los diversos colectivos.

Il a été prouvé que des toilettes bien conçues favorisent la communication et améliorent l'ambiance au travail, augmentant de cette façon le rendement des employés. En même temps, cela met en relief les valeurs propres à l'entreprise et apporte des informations sur le secteur de production de celle-ci. Les projets analysés dans ce paragraphe en sont la preuve: des toilettes appartenant à des entreprises, à des bureaux, à des magasins, à des showrooms et à des centres commerciaux proposent un design fonctionnel et visuellement attrayant tout spécialement adaptés aux besoins des différents utilisateurs.

Het is bewezen dat een goede toiletruimte de communicatie op het werk verbetert en bovendien een gunstige invloed heeft op de werksfeer, hetgeen weer bijdraagt aan een hogere productie van de werknemers. Tegelijkertijd is het sanitair het visitekaartje van een bedrijf. De volgende voorbeelden betreffen toiletten in kantoren, winkels, showrooms en winkelcentra die zijn ontworpen volgens bovenstaande principes. De designs zijn functioneel, visueel aantrekkelijk en bovendien aangepast aan de behoeften van de verschillende gebruikersgroepen.

VALTECH

This electronic business consultancy includes a unisex bathroom with walls covered in mirrors that serve to expand the space, eliminate barriers and immerse the user in a world of fantasy and adventure. The mirrors create the impression of an almost infinite extension of space, while a series of photomontages transport the user from the depths of the oceans to the heights of Alpine meadows.

Gli uffici di questa agenzia di consulenza, specializzata nel settore dell'e-commerce, includono un bagno unisex con pareti ricoperte da specchi la cui funzione è di ampliare lo spazio, eliminare frontiere e immergere l'utente in un mondo fantastico e avventuroso. Gli specchi danno l'impressione di un'estensione quasi infinita dello spazio; una serie di fotomontaggi trasporta gli utenti dalle profondità degli oceani alle verdi distese alpine.

Esta consultoría de comercio electrónico incluye un baño unisex con paredes cubiertas por espejos cuya función es ampliar el espacio, eliminar fronteras y sumergir al usuario en un mundo de fantasía y aventura. Los espejos le proporcionan la impresión de una extensión casi infinita del espacio, a la vez que una serie de fotomontajes lo trasladan desde las profundidades de los océanos hasta las praderas alpinas.

Cette agence conseil en commerce électronique a des toilettes unisexes avec des parois recouvertes de verre dont la fonction est d'agrandir l'espace, d'éliminer les frontières et de faire pénétrer l'utilisateur dans un monde de fantaisie et d'aventure. Les miroirs donnent l'impression d'une extension presque infinie de l'espace ; une série de photomontages font voyager ceux qui s'en servent des profondeurs de l'océan aux prairies alpines.

Dit adviesbureau voor elektronische handel beschikt over unisekssanitair met spiegelwanden die de ruimte vergroten en grenzen doen vervagen. De gebruikers worden ondergedompeld in een wereld vol fantasie en avontuur. Door de spiegels lijkt de ruimte bijna oneindig en de fotomontages van oceaanbodems en Alpenweiden versterken het gevoel van grenzeloosheid.

Architect: Harper Mackay
Photography: Chris Gascoigne/View
Location: London, UK

NISSAN HEADQUARTERS

More than buying a product, in this Nissan showroom the visitor acquires an understanding of the company's philosophy. Situated on one of Tokyo's most famous streets, right in the city center, this space of extraordinarily limited dimensions – no more than two cars can fit inside – bestows a capital importance on its bathrooms, which convey the values of Nissan by expressing modernity, purity, functionality and elegance.

Lo showroom di Nissan ha una funzione che va al di là di quella puramente commerciale. Infatti, pur non acquistando nessun prodotto, il visitatore che vi entra comprende la filosofia dell'azienda. Situato in una delle strade più note di Tokyo, questo spazio dalle dimensioni straordinariamente ridotte dà un'importanza capitale ai suoi bagni, accurato mezzo di espressione dei valori di modernità, purezza, funzionalità ed eleganza.

Más que comprar un producto, en el showroom de Nissan el visitante adquiere conocimiento de la filosofía de la empresa. Situado en una de las calles más conocidas de Tokio, este espacio de dimensiones extraordinariamente reducidas da una importancia capital a sus baños, que transmiten los valores de modernidad, pureza, funcionalidad y elegancia.

Dans le showroom de Nissan, plus que d'acheter un produit, le visiteur fait connaissance avec la philosophie de l'entreprise. Situé dans une des rues plus connues de Tokyo, en plein centre ville, cet espace aux dimensions très réduites – il n'y a pas la place pour deux véhicules – donne une importance capitale à ses toilettes ; elles transmettent de cette sorte les valeurs de Nissan, c'est à dire la modernité, la pureté, la fonctionnalité et l'élégance.

In de showroom van Nissan gaat het niet zozeer om de verkoop van een product als wel om het overbrengen van de filosofie van het bedrijf. Gevestigd in een van de bekendste straten van Tokio, midden in het centrum van de stad, biedt deze kleine showroom slechts ruimte aan twee auto's. Het sanitair wint daarmee sterk aan belang en verbeeldt de waarden die Nissan wil uitdragen: moderniteit, functionaliteit en elegantie.

Architect: Fumita Design Office
Year: 2001
Photography: Nacása & Partners Inc.
Location: Tokyo, Japan

Light takes on an unprecedented importance in a bathroom that confronts the visitor with a futuristic setting in which the use of traditional materials leads to innovative and original solutions. Smooth surfaces are combined with textured walls and the most brightly lit areas are softened with steel, which absorbs any excess of luminosity.

La luce acquista un'importanza senza precedenti in un bagno che si presenta al visitatore come uno spazio futurista, dove l'uso di materiali tradizionali porta a soluzioni innovative e originali. Superfici lisce si abbinano a pareti con diverse strutture, e le parti più illuminate vengono attenuate mediante l'acciaio, materiale in grado di assorbire l'eccesso di luminosità.

La luz adquiere una importancia sin precedentes en un baño que se presenta al visitante como un espacio futurista en el que el empleo de materiales tradicionales lleva a soluciones innovadoras y originales. Superficies lisas se combinan con paredes con texturas y las partes más iluminadas se suavizan con acero que absorbe el exceso de luminosidad.

La lumière prend une importance sans précédent dans des toilettes qui sont présentées aux visiteurs comme un espace futuriste dans lesquelles l'emploi de matériaux traditionnels amène à des solutions innovatrices et originales. Des surfaces lisses sont combinées aux murs recouverts de tissus et les parties les plus éclairées sont adoucies grâce à l'emploi d'acier qui absorbe l'excès de luminosité.

Het licht speelt een hoofdrol in deze futuristische wc waarin traditionele materialen op een innovatieve en originele wijze zijn toegepast. Gladde oppervlakken worden gecombineerd met wanden met meer textuur en in de meest verlichte delen is staal verwerkt waardoor het teveel aan licht wordt geabsorbeerd.

SHOWROOM BISAZZA

For the showroom of the Bisazza company in Berlin, the architect Fabio Novembre drew on Samuel Beckett's play *Waiting for Godot*, which he interpreted as a synthesis between opposing cultures and realities that are also reflected in the bathroom. A spectacular setting unfurls in the interior, where a large double-faced mask made of gleaming steel and golden mosaic stands as a symbol of opposites.

Per lo showroom dell'azienda vicentina Bisazza a Berlino, l'estroso architetto Fabio Novembre si è ispirato al testo di Samuel Beckett *Aspettando Godot* interpretato come una sintesi tra culture e realtà opposte che si riflette anche nella stanza da bagno. All'interno dello showroom prende forma una spettacolare scenografia con una grande maschera a doppia faccia, simbolo degli opposti, realizzata in acciaio brillante e mosaico dorato.

Para el showroom de la firma Bisazza en Berlín, el arquitecto Fabio Novembre se inspiró en el texto de Samuel Beckett *Esperando a Godot*, que interpretó como una síntesis entre culturas y realidades opuestas que se refleja también en el baño. Una espectacular escenografía se desarrolla en el espacio interior, donde un gran antifaz de doble cara, de acero brillante y en mosaico dorado se levanta como símbolo de los opuestos.

Pour le showroom de la firme Bisazza à Berlin, l'architecte Fabio Novembre s'est inspiré du texte de Samuel Beckett "en attendant Godot" qu'il a interprété comme une synthèse entre cultures et réalités opposées. Cette interprétation se reflète aussi dans les toilettes. Une mise en scène spectaculaire est proposée dans l'espace intérieur, où un grand masque à double face, en acier brillant et en mosaïque dorée, se lève comme un symbole des opposés.

Samuel Beckett's *Wachten op Godot* vormde de inspiratiebron voor architect Fabio Novembre bij het ontwerp van de showroom van de firma Bisazza in Berlijn. Hij interpreteerde de tekst als een sinthese tussen tegengestelde culturen en werkelijkheden, hetgeen ook wordt weerspiegeld in het wc-ontwerp. In het interieur bevindt zich een spectaculair decor waarbij een groot masker met twee gezichten, glimmend staal en goudkleurig mozaïek, de twee tegenpolen symboliseert.

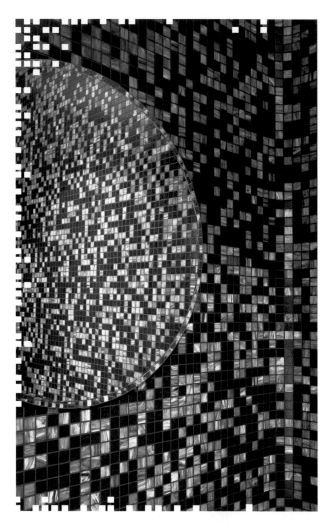

Architect: Fabio Novembre
Year: 2003
Photography: Alberto Ferrero
Location: Berlin, Germany

Between appearence and reality, life and theater, the spiritual and material, the visitor relives the dialogues between Vladimir and Estragon as they are waiting for Godot.

Tra apparenza e realtà, vita e teatro, spiritualità e materialismo, il visitatore rivive il dialogo tra Vladimir ed Estragon, nell'attesa che arrivi Godot.

Entre apariencia y realidad, vida y teatro, espiritual y material, el visitante revive el diálogo entre Vladimiro y Estragón esperando a Godot.

Entre apparence et réalité, vie et théâtre, spirituel et matériel, le visiteur revit le dialogue entre Vladimir et Estragon en attendant Godot.

Tussen schijn en werkelijkheid, leven en theater, geest en materie beleeft de toiletganger de dialoog tussen Vladimir en Estragon die wachten op Godot.

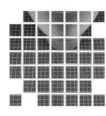

GeBERIT TRAINING CENTER

The Designrichtung studio conceived the passage through the new training center for Geberit, the Swiss bath manufacturer, as a journey. The visitor goes down a cold, poorly lit corridor – an esthetic aspect frequently associated with public lavatories – then moves through a curtain of water modulated by a remote control and reaches a second corridor inundated with colors and aromas.

Per il nuovo centro di formazione del produttore di bagni svizzero Geberit, lo studio di architettura Designrichtung ha concepito il percorso all'interno della toilette come un viaggio. Il visitatore si sposta lungo un corridoio scarsamente illuminato e freddo – estetica frequentemente associata ai servizi pubblici – poi passa attraverso una tendina d'acqua controllata con un telecomando, e arriva a un secondo corridoio inondato da colori e profumi.

Para el nuevo centro de formación del fabricante de baños suizos Geberit, el estudio Designrichtung concibió el recorrido por el espacio como un viaje. El visitante se desplaza por un pasillo pobremente iluminado y frío, estética frecuentemente asociada a los servicios públicos, pasa a continuación a través de una cortina de agua dirigida por control remoto y llega a un segundo corredor inundado por colores y perfumes.

Pour le nouveau centre de formation du fabricant suisse de salles de bain Geberit, le studio Designrichtung a conçu un parcours dans l'espace comme s'il s'agissait d'un voyage. Le visiteur se déplace dans un couloir faiblement éclairé et froid, esthétique couramment associée aux toilettes publiques, passe ensuite à travers un rideau d'eau dirigé par contrôle à distance et arrive dans un second couloir inondé de couleurs et de parfums.

Voor het nieuwe opleidingscentrum van de Zwitserse badkamerfabrikant Geberit heeft Designrichtung een toiletruimte ontworpen die als een spannende reis is. Eerst moet de bezoeker door een slechtverlichte, kille gang, die doet denken aan de gangbare toiletesthetiek. Vervolgens betreedt hij via een op afstand bediend watergordijn een tweede gang die baadt in licht en geuren.

Architect: Designrichtung
Year: 2003
Photography: Tom Bisig
Location: Jona, Switzerland

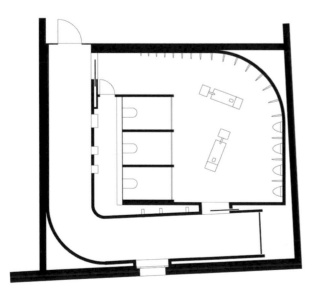

Floor plan

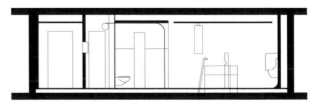

Section

The bathroom area is conceived as a hi-tech space in which all the equipment operate automatically: the doors to the cubicles are activated by sensors and the video sequences, projected on to the urinals, change as the user approaches the compartments, creating an artistic innovation that is in constant evolution.

L'area del bagno si delinea come uno spazio decisamente *high tech* dove tutte le apparecchiature sono automatiche. Le porte di accesso ai cubicoli vengono attivate da appositi sensori, e le sequenze video proiettate sopra gli orinatoi cambiano man mano che l'utente si avvicina agli scomparti: una vera innovazione artistica in costante evoluzione.

El área del baño se configura como un espacio de alta tecnología en el que todas las acciones se activan automáticamente: las puertas de los cubículos se activan por sensores y las secuencias de vídeo proyectadas sobre los urinales cambian a medida que el usuario se acerca a los compartimentos y conforman una instalación artística en constante evolución.

La zone des toilettes a été pensée comme un espace de haute technologie dans lequel tout est automatique ; les portes des W.C. s'activent par des senseurs et les séquences de vidéo projetées au-dessous des urinoirs changent au fur et à mesure que l'utilisateur s'approche d'eux, créant une installation artistique en constante évolution.

Het wc-gedeelte is hightech waarbij alle faciliteiten automatisch werken zonder enig handwerk. De deuren naar de toiletten openen via sensoren en de videobeelden die worden geprojecteerd op de urinoirs veranderen als de gebruiker dichterbij komt.

SICIS SHOWROOM

This mosaic company has christened its new showroom in Milan, the Art Factory. Designed by Marco Piva in collaboration with artists like Tom Dixon, Patricia Urquiola, Ora Ito and Jordi Labanda, the space is a mixture of colors and forms whose principal means of expression is the mosaic. The bathrooms are a continuation of the showroom and feature areas covered with some of the firm's mosaics.

The Art Factory (la fabbrica dell'arte): è lo slogan che accompagna tutti i prodotti della nota azienda ravennate di mosaici. Il suo nuovo showroom di Milano è stato progettato da Marco Piva in collaborazione con artisti come Tom Dixon, Patricia Urquiola, Ora Ito e Jordi Labanda. Lo spazio si caratterizza per l'uso di vari colori e volumi. Sulla stessa linea dello showroom, i bagni mostrano superfici accuratamente rivestite da mosaici di loro produzione.

The Art Factory (fábrica de arte), así denomina la empresa de mosaicos su nuevo showroom en Milán. Diseñado por Marco Piva en colaboración con artistas como Tom Dixon, Patricia Urquiola, Ora Ito o Jordi Labanda, el espacio es una mezcla de colores y volúmenes. Los lavabos continúan el showroom y muestran superficies recubiertas con mosaicos de la firma.

The Art Factory (l'usine de l'art), c'est ainsi que l'entreprise de mosaïque surnomme son nouveau showroom à Milan. Designé par Marco Piva en collaboration avec des artistes comme Tom Dixon, Patricia Urquiola, Ora Ito ou Jordi Labanda, l'espace est un mélange de couleurs et de volumes dont la forme d'expression se concentre sur la mosaïque. Les toilettes sont la suite du showroom et montrent des surfaces recouvertes par les mosaïques de la firme.

"De Kunstfabriek", zo noemt dit mozaïekbedrijf zijn nieuwe showroom in Milaan. De ruimte, ontworpen door Marco Piva in samenwerking met kunstenaars als Tom Dixon, Patricia Urquiola, Ora Ito en Jordi Labanda, is een mengeling van kleuren en volumes uitgedrukt in mozaïekwerk. De wc's sluiten aan op het ontwerp van de rest van de showroom en zijn bedekt met mozaïeken van SICIS.

Architect: Marco Piva
Year: 2004
Photography: Maurizio Marcato
Location: Milan, Italy

As they run across the surfaces of the bathroom, the Sicis mosaics trace geometric designs that turn the space into a jigsaw of various colors and forms.

Lungo le superfici della zona servizi, i mosaici Sicis tracciano disegni geometrici che convertono lo spazio in un puzzle di colori e forme diverse.

En su recorrido por las superficies del cuarto de baño, los mosaicos de Sicis trazan dibujos geométricos que convierten el espacio en un puzzle de colores y formas diversas.

Dans leur parcours sur les surfaces de la salle de bain, les mosaïques de Sicis tracent des dessins géométriques qui transforment l'espace en un puzzle de couleurs et de formes diverses.

De oppervlakken van het toilet zijn eveneens belegd met geometrische mozaïeken die de ruimte veranderen in een puzzel van verschillende kleuren en vormen.

oRANGE BUILDING

The bathroom is traditionally considered a merely functional space, lacking in visual attraction or allure. Starting with the premise that informality and relaxation inspire creativity, and that the latter encourages the exchange of ideas, this architecture studio sought to promote communication through its most common tool: the word, present in each and every corner of the toilets.

Tradizionalmente il bagno viene associato a un ambiente meramente funzionale, privo di attrattive e stimoli visuali. Partendo dal presupposto che la disinvoltura e il relax alimentano la creatività, e che questa a sua volta propizia lo scambio di idee, lo studio di architettura N. Grimshaw & Partners ha cercato di promuovere la comunicazione attraverso il suo strumento più comune: la parola, presente in tutti gli angoli della toilette.

El lavabo se asocia tradicionalmente a un espacio meramente funcional, carente de atractivos y alicientes visuales. Partiendo de la base de que el desenfado y la relajación alimentan la creatividad, y que ésta fomenta el intercambio de ideas, el estudio de arquitectura pretende promover la comunicación a través de su herramienta más común: la palabra, presente en todos y cada uno de los rincones de los inodoros.

Les toilettes sont traditionnellement associées à un espace purement fonctionnel, manquant d'attraits et de stimulants visuels. En partant du concept que le confort et la relaxation alimentent la créativité, et que celle-ci favorise l'échange des idées, l'atelier d'architecture cherche à promouvoir la communication grâce à son outil le plus commun : la parole, présente dans tous les recoins des W.C.

De wc wordt van oudsher geassocieerd met een functionele ruimte zonder visuele aantrekkingskracht. Vanuit het idee dat rust en ontspanning de creativiteit voeden, wat weer leidt tot een uitwisseling van ideeën, wil dit architectenbureau de communicatie bevorderen via haar belangrijkste werktuig: het woord, dat aanwezig is in alle hoeken van de toiletten.

Architect: Nicholas Grimshaw & Partners
Photography: Peter Cook/ View
Location: Darlington, UK

DURAVIT SPAIN

The design of the new logistical headquarters and offices of the Duravit company, used a green color treated with resin to cover every surface. The bright lighting gives pride of place to the minimalist space without focusing on any auxiliary elements. Instead, these have been picked out by indirect lighting derived from the creation of skylights pointing toward the walls.

Per la realizzazione della nuova sede logistica e degli uffici della ditta Duravit, si è optato per il colore verde trattato con resina per rivestire tutte le superfici. L'intensa illuminazione rende protagonista il minimalismo dello spazio senza mettere in luce elementi accessori. Per questo si è preferito usare un'illuminazione indiretta, ottenuta mediante la creazione di faretti rivolti verso le pareti.

En el diseño de la nueva sede logística y de las oficinas de la firma Duravit, se ha utilizado el color verde tratado con resina para recubrir todas las superficies. La iluminación, intensa, da protagonismo al espacio minimalista sin que destaquen los elementos auxiliares. Para ello se ha optado por una iluminación indirecta obtenida mediante focos de luz cenital dirigidos hacia las paredes.

Dans le design du nouveau siège logistique et des bureaux de la firme Duravit, on a utilisé la couleur verte traitée avec de la résine pour recouvrir toutes les surfaces. L'éclairage intense donne de l'importance à cet espace minimaliste sans que les éléments auxiliaires s'en détachent. On a donc opté pour un éclairage indirect obtenu en créant des illuminations zénithales dirigées vers les parois.

In het ontwerp van de nieuwe logistieke zetel en de kantoren van de firma Duravit, is de kleur groen gebruikt om alle oppervlakken te bedekken. De felle lampen zetten deze minimalistische ruimte in de schijnwerpers zonder zelf op de voorgrond te treden. Daarom is gekozen voor indirecte verlichting via spotjes in het plafond gericht op de muren.

Architect: Francesc Rifé
Year: 2004
Photography: Eugeni Pons
Location: Barcelona, Spain

GIORGIO ARMANI BOUTIQUE

The large dimensions of the space and the quality of the materials give this bathroom an ethereal atmosphere that is enriched by the diffuse light. The ceramics of the washbasin are complemented by a dark, wooden surface that runs throughout the space, stripped bare of details. The choice of materials was determined by the warmth and spatial uniformity achieved by the combination of wood and other opaque materials.

L'ampiezza e la qualità dei materiali conferiscono a questo bagno un aspetto etereo che viene arricchito da una luce tenue. La ceramica del lavabo si abbina a una superficie in legno dal tono scuro che percorre lo spazio austero, privo di particolari. La scelta dei materiali è stata determinata dal loro calore e dall'uniformità spaziale, ottenuta mediante l'accostamento del legno e di altri materiali opachi.

La amplitud de espacio y la calidad de los materiales transforman este baño en un ambiente etéreo que se enriquece con una luz tenue. La piedra cerámica del lavamanos se combina con una superficie de madera de un tono oscuro que recorre el espacio, parco en detalles. La elección de los materiales se ha regido por la calidez y la uniformidad espacial conseguida a partir de la combinación de maderas y otros materiales opacos.

L'amplitude de l'espace et la qualité des matériaux confèrent à ces toilettes une ambiance éthérée qui s'enrichit avec une lumière tamisée. Dans un espace qui ne s'embarrasse pas de détails, la pierre céramique du lavabo est combinée à une surface en bois d'un ton foncé. Le choix des matériaux a été régi par la qualité et l'espace est rendu uniforme grâce à la combinaison de différents bois et de matériaux opaques.

De weidsheid van de ruimte en de kwaliteit van de gebruikte materialen geven dit sanitair een hemels uiterlijk wat nog wordt versterkt door het versluierde lichtgebruik. Het keramiek van de wastafels is gecombineerd met een oppervlak van donker hout dat ook in de rest van de strak uitgevoerde ruimte wordt gebruikt. De opake materialen zijn uitgekozen vanwege hun warme uitstraling en om ruimtelijke eenheid te creëren.

Architect: Claudio Silvestrin Architects
Photography: Matteo Piazza
Location: Milan, Italy

The crushed-stone floor and the smooth structure enrich the uniformity of the space, characterized by its simplicity and tastefulness.

Il pavimento in graniglia e la struttura liscia arricchiscono l'uniformità dello spazio, caratterizzato dalla semplicità e dall'ordine.

El suelo de grava y la estructura lisa enriquecen la uniformidad del espacio, caracterizado por la sencillez y la pulcritud.

Le sol en gravier et la structure lisse enrichissent l'uniformité de l'espace qui se caractérise par la simplicité et la netteté.

De grindvloer en de tot in de puntjes verzorgde afwerking vergroten deze uniformiteit van de ruimte nog verder.

SWISS RE HEADQUARTERS

The design for the bathrooms of these offices revolves around the idea of combining employees' autonomy with the feeling of belonging to a group. To achieve this, a space that is basically narrow was widened visually by inserting a glass façade that lets in the sunlight, and by using pastel colors, which are always useful when it comes to enlarging a space of limited dimensions.

Il design delle toilette di questi uffici ruota attorno all'idea di combinare l'autonomia dei lavoratori con un senso di appartenenza a un gruppo. È così che uno spazio originariamente stretto si dilata visivamente, grazie a una vetrata che lascia passare la luce naturale e all'uso di toni pastello, sempre adatti a ingrandire un vano di dimensioni ridotte.

El diseño de los lavabos de estas oficinas gira en torno a la idea de combinar la autonomía de los trabajadores con un sentimiento de pertenencia a un grupo. Para ello, un espacio en principio estrecho se dilata visualmente gracias a la inclusión de una fachada acristalada, que permite la entrada de luz natural, y al empleo de tonos pastel, siempre útiles a la hora de agrandar una estancia de dimensiones reducidas.

Le design des toilettes de ces bureaux tourne autour de l'idée de combiner l'autonomie des employés au sentiment d'appartenance à un groupe. A cette fin, un espace étroit se dilate visuellement grâce à une façade en verre qui permet de laisser entrer la lumière naturelle et à l'emploi de tons pastel toujours utiles lorsqu'on veut agrandir une pièce de dimensions réduites.

Het ontwerp van de toiletten van dit kantoor is gebaseerd op het idee om de autonomie van de werknemers te versterken en ze tegelijkertijd het gevoel te geven dat ze deel uitmaken van een grotere groep. Daarom wordt de in principe vrij nauwe ruimte visueel vergroot door het gebruik van een glazen wand die natuurlijk licht doorlaat en het gebruik van pasteltinten, wat altijd goed werkt om een kleine ruimte groter te doen lijken.

Architect: Bothe Richter Teherani
Year: 2001
Photography: Jörg Hempel/Photodesign
Location: Munich, Germany

DOCTOR SCHEDLE OFFICE

The bathrooms in Dr. Schedle's office have the effect of making any patient feel protected. The cool blue tones combined with dim lights, and pure linear forms of the fixtures are visually relaxing, alleviating the sensation of anxiety commonly experienced during a visit to the doctor.

Nella toilette dello studio del dottor Schedle, il paziente che si trovi nella necessità di usare il bagno sperimenterà una sensazione di tranquillità. I toni freddi dell'azzurro, attenuati da una luce soffusa, e le linee rette e pure dei sanitari hanno un effetto visualmente rilassante e riducono l'ansia che può accompagnare il paziente quando si sottopone a una visita medica.

En la consulta del Dr. Schedle, el paciente que haga uso de los excusados se sentirá arropado por una sensación de confianza. Las tonalidades frías del azul, matizadas por una luz tenue, y las líneas rectas y puras de los sanitarios actúan como relajante visual y aminoran la sensación de incomodidad que suele generar una visita al médico.

Dans la consultation du Docteur Schedle, le patient qui entre dans la toilette poudra voir un design qui réussit à donner une sensation de confiance. La gamme froide des bleus nuancée par une lumière faible, et les lignes droites et pures de ses éléments sont un relaxant visuel qui font de la salle des bains un espace qui diminue l'incommodité que peut générer une visite médicale.

In de praktijk van dokter Schedle ervaart de patiënt die het toilet gebruikt een weldadige rust. De frisse blauwtinten, versluierd door het zachte licht, zorgen in combinatie met de rechte en pure lijnen voor visuele ontspanning. Hierdoor voelen de mensen zich meer op hun gemak tijdens hun doktersbezoek.

Architect: Eichinger oder Knechtl
Year: 2002
Photography: Margherita Spiluttini
Location: Vienna, Austria

MARKS & SPENCER STORE

The bathrooms in the new Marks & Spencer store reflect the aims of a company determined to extend its clientele to a younger public in tune with the latest fashions. In accordance with this objective, the bathrooms create a colorful, pop-art atmosphere that exudes freshness, modernity and cleanliness. The ensemble is made up of two unisex toilets and a bathroom for disabled customers, and it also incorporates facilities for changing diapers.

I bagni del nuovo negozio Marks & Spencer rispecchiano gli obiettivi della compagnia, decisa ad ampliare la sua clientela verso un pubblico più giovane e attento alla moda. In linea con questo obiettivo, i bagni ricreano un ambiente colorato e pop che sprizza freschezza, modernità e lucentezza. L'intera unità si compone di due servizi unisex, un bagno per disabili e un'area per il cambio dei pannolini.

Los lavabos de la nueva tienda Marks & Spencer reflejan los objetivos de la compañía, decidida a ampliar su clientela a un público más joven y orientado a la moda. De acuerdo con este objetivo, los baños recrean un ambiente colorido y pop que destila frescura, modernidad y limpieza. El conjunto está compuesto por dos servicios unisex y un lavabo para minusválidos, y un espacio reservado para el cambio de pañales del bebé.

Les toilettes du nouveau magasin Marks & Spencer reflètent les objectifs de la compagnie décidée à élargir sa clientèle à un public plus jeune et intéressé par la mode. En accord avec ces objectifs, les toilettes recréent une ambiance colorée et pop d'où se dégagent fraîcheur, modernité et propreté. L'ensemble se compose de deux W.C. unisexes et d'un lavabo pour handicapés physiques ; il dispose également d'un espace pour changer les couches des bébés.

Het sanitair van deze nieuwe vestiging van Marks & Spencer weerspiegelt de doelstelling van dit winkelbedrijf om zijn markt uit te breiden naar een jonger en modegevoelig publiek. De wc's zijn kleurig en hip en hebben een frisse, moderne en schone uitstraling. Het complex omvat twee unisekstoiletten, een aparte ruimte voor lichamelijk gehandicapten en een luiertafel.

Architect: Urban Salon
Year: 2004
Photography: Sue Barr/View
Location: Speke, UK

NA**R**DINI

The public bathrooms in this Italian distillery are set behind an entrance tiled with white mosaic. The interior has a light touch, thanks to the use of soft colors and glass surfaces which contrast with the warmth of the Iroko wood flooring. The quality of the light and the delicate simplicity of the structure clash with the reinforced concrete featured in some elements of the interior.

Dietro l'ingresso rivestito di mosaico bianco, si trovano i servizi pubblici di questa distilleria italiana. L'interno si presenta con un tocco leggero grazie all'uso di colori morbidi e di superfici vetrate, che contrastano con i toni caldi del pavimento realizzato in legno iroko. La qualità della luce, l'immaterialità e la semplicità della struttura sono messi a confronto con il cemento armato di alcuni elementi dell'interno.

Tras la entrada revestida con mosaico blanco, se encuentran los baños públicos de esta destilería italiana. El interior se presenta como un volumen liviano gracias al uso de colores suaves y de superficies acristaladas que contrastan con la calidez del pavimento de madera de iroko. La calidad de la luz, la inmaterialidad y la sencillez de la estructura se confrontan con el cemento armado de algunos elementos del interior.

Derrière l'entrée revétue de mosaïque blanche se trouvent les toilettes publiques de cette distillerie italienne. L'intérieur se présente comme un volume allégé grâce à l'utilisation de couleurs douces et de surfaces en verre qui contrastent avec le côté chaud transmis par le parquet en bois d'iroko. La qualité de la lumière, l'immatérialité et la simplicité de la structure sont confrontées au béton armé de certains éléments de l'intérieur.

Achter een met wit mozaïek bekleed halletje bevinden zich de wc's van dit Italiaanse destilleerbedrijf. Het interieur is licht dankzij het gebruik van zachte kleuren en glaswerk, die contrasteren met de warmte van de houten vloer. Het mooie lichtgebruik, de lichte materialen en eenvoudige structuren zijn ook in tegenspraak met enkele betonnen elementen in het interieur.

Architect: Massimiliano Fuksas
Year: 2004
Photography: Maurizio Marcato
Location: Bassano del Grappa, Italy

WINE STORE

The main focus of interest in this bathroom of limited dimensions is the handling of the washbasin area: it stands apart from the rest of the space through the predominance of polished metal, which sets up gleaming reflections and provides a modern touch. All the objects here, from the washbasins themselves to the faucets and soap dispenser, are made of this material.

L'interesse principale di questo bagno dalle ridotte dimensioni consiste nel fatto che il lavabo si trova in una zona a parte rispetto al resto. Il metallo lucido è il protagonista di quest'area: dota le varie superfici di riflessi e luccichii che conferiscono al complesso un aspetto di modernità. Tutti gli oggetti, dal lavabo fino ai rubinetti e al dispenser per il sapone, sono stati realizzati in questo materiale.

El interés principal de este baño de reducidas dimensiones reside en el tratamiento de la zona donde se ubica el lavamanos, en oposición al resto del espacio. El metal pulido es el protagonista de esta área, ya que dota a las superficies de brillos y reflejos que confieren modernidad al conjunto. Todos los objetos, desde el lavamanos hasta la grifería y el dispensador de jabón, son de este material.

L'espace où se trouve le lavabo s'oppose au reste du lieu. C'est là le principal intérêt de ces toilettes aux dimensions réduites. Ici, le métal poli domine. Il donne aux surfaces des aspects brillants et des reflets qui confèrent modernité à l'ensemble. Tous les objets, du lavabo à la robinetterie, en passant par le distributeur de savon, sont fabriqués dans ce matériau.

Het meest in het oog springende detail van dit kleine toilet is het wastafelgedeelte dat een contrast vormt met de rest van de ruimte. Het gepolijste metaal vervult een hoofdrol in dit gebied en de glans en weerspiegeling zorgen voor een moderne uitstraling. Alle voorzieningen, van de wastafel tot de kraan en de zeepdispenser, zijn gemaakt van dit materiaal.

Architect: Gasparin & Meier
Photography: Margherita Spiluttini
Location: Klagefurt, Austria

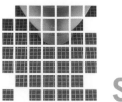

SIEMENS HEADQUARTERS

The bathrooms in the Siemens headquarters in Switzerland reflect a concern to cater to the needs of the company's workforce. So, a colorful, modern-looking setting has been created to transform the bathroom into a pleasant, cheerful and positive space that transcends the usual functional approach. The bathroom becomes a medium capable of enhancing not only its users' well-being but also their emotional state.

I bagni della sede centrale della Siemens in Svizzera riflettono la preoccupazione dell'azienda di dare una risposta alle esigenze dei lavoratori: lo spazio presenta un ambiente colorato e moderno che trasforma il bagno in un luogo piacevole, ameno ed ottimista che trascende la solita impostazione funzionale. Il bagno diventa uno strumento in grado di suscitare il benessere non solo fisico, ma anche emozionale degli utenti.

Los baños de la sede de Siemens en Suiza reflejan una preocupación por dar respuesta a las necesidades de los trabajadores. En este sentido, el espacio configura un ambiente colorido y moderno que transforma el lavabo en un lugar agradable, divertido y optimista, y trasciende el habitual enfoque funcional. El baño se convierte en un medio capaz de suscitar el bienestar no sólo físico, sino también emocional de los usuarios.

Les toilettes du siège social de Siemens, en Suisse, cherchent à répondre aux attentes des employés. L'espace propose une ambiance colorée et moderne qui transforme ces toilettes en un lieu agréable, amusant et positif. Elles transmettent un bien-être physique et émotionnel à leur utilisateurs.

De toiletten van het hoofdkwartier van Siemens in Zwitserland beantwoorden aan de wensen van de werknemers. Het zijn kleurige en moderne ruimtes, die functioneel zijn maar toch een aangename en optimistische uitstraling hebben. De wc is hiermee een medium dat in staat is om niet alleen het fysieke welzijn van de gebruiker te verbeteren, maar ook het emotionele.

Architect: Camenzind Evolution
Year: 2002
Photography: Peter Wurmli
Location: Zurich, Switzerland

PALAIS EQUITABLE

This public bathroom was developed from a series of open spaces with pure lines and polished surfaces. A sliding door makes the bathroom area independent of the entrance without obstructing its visibility. The flooring in the entrance has been covered with natural wood, while that of the interior has been treated with the same color as the walls and ceiling to create a monochrome space that sets off the washbasin.

Questo bagno pubblico si sviluppa a partire da una serie di volumi aperti dalle linee pure e dalle superfici levigate. Una porta scorrevole rende indipendente la zona del bagno dall'entrata, senza interrompere però la visibilità. Il pavimento dell'entrata è stato realizzato in legno naturale, mentre quello dell'interno è stato trattato con lo stesso colore delle pareti e del soffitto, al fine di ottenere un volume monocromatico su cui spicca il lavabo.

Este baño público se desarrolla a partir de una serie de volúmenes abiertos de líneas puras y superficies pulidas. Una puerta corredera separa la zona del baño de la entrada sin interrumpir la visibilidad. El pavimento de la entrada se ha cubierto con madera natural, mientras que el del interior ha sido tratado con el mismo color que las paredes y el techo para lograr un volumen monocromático donde destaca un lavamanos.

Ces toilettes publiques ont été conçues à partir d'une série de volumes ouverts, de lignes pures et de surfaces polies. Une porte coulissante sépare la zone des toilettes de l'entrée sans interrompre la visibilité. Le parquet de l'entrée a été réalisé avec du bois naturel, et celui de l'intérieur a été traité avec la même couleur que les murs et le plafond pour obtenir un volume monochromatique dans lequel se détache un lavabo.

Dit openbare toilet is ontwikkeld in een open ruimte met pure lijnen en gepolijste oppervlakken. Een schuifdeur zorgt ervoor dat afscheiding mogelijk is zonder dat de doorgaande lijn wordt doorbroken. De vloer van het voorportaal is van hout gemaakt, terwijl de vloer van de wc's zelf dezelfde kleur heeft als de wanden en het plafond waardoor een monochromatische ruimte ontstaat waarin de wasbak op de voorgrond treedt.

Architect: Rüdiger Lainer
Year: 1997
Photography: Margherita Spiluttini
Location: Vienna, Austria

NORTON ROSE VIEREGGE

These urinals, designed by Starck and Duravit, form part of the offices of Norton Rose Vieregge. The white marble creates an impression of both luxury and coldness, which is relieved by rose petals placed in the glass receptacles fitted into the wall. The petals provide the only splash of color in a setting marked by an austere sobriety that is unexpected but nevertheless eye-catching.

Questi orinatoi, disegnati da Starck e Duravit, fanno parte degli uffici dello studio legale Norton Rose Vieregge. Il marmo bianco crea una sensazione di eleganza e al contempo di freddezza, dissimulata da alcuni petali di rosa collocati in recipienti di vetro inseriti nella parete. I petali sono l'unica nota di colore in un ambiente dalla sobrietà cromatica sorprendente, che malgrado tutto è in grado di colpire l'attenzione.

Estos urinarios, diseñados por Starck y Duravit, forman parte de las oficinas de Norton Rose Vieregge. El mármol blanco produce una impresión que es a la vez de lujo y frialdad, y que es paliada por unos pétalos de rosa colocados en recipientes de cristal e integrados en la pared. Los pétalos son la única nota de color en un ambiente de una sobriedad cromática sorprendente, que no por eso deja de atraer las miradas.

Ces urinoirs, designés par Starck et Duravit, font partie des bureaux de Norton Rose Vieregge. Le marbre blanc produit à la fois une impression de luxe et de froideur, atténuée par des pétales de roses placées dans des récipients en verre intégrés dans le mur. Les pétales sont la seule note de couleur dans une ambiance d'une sobriété chromatique surprenante mais qui attire tout de même les regards.

Deze door Starck en Duravit ontworpen urinoirs maken deel uit van het kantoorcomplex van Norton Rose Vieregge. Het witte marmer heeft tegelijkertijd een luxueuze en kille uitstraling wat verzacht wordt door de rozenblaadjes die in glazen houdertjes in de wand zijn geplaatst. Deze bloemblaadjes vormen het enige kleuraccent in deze opvallend sobere ruimte die desondanks een aantrekkelijke aanblik biedt.

Architect: 100% Interior
Year: 2001
Photography: Karin Heßmann
Location: Frankfurt, Germany

MINISTUDIO IN PARIS

Leonardo Anecca's studio has transformed a dark, poky storage area into a cheerful, welcoming bathroom. The installation of a shower right in the center of the narrow room took full advantage of the available space, while proving an optimal solution for people who make use of the bathroom's other functions only occasionally. A series of adjustable lights can be regulated in accordance with the desires of the user.

Lo studio di Leonardo Anecca ha trasformato un angolo scuro, originariamente adibito a ripostiglio, in un bagno accogliente e ameno. Una delle soluzioni adottate per sfruttare al meglio lo spazio è stata l'installazione di una doccia proprio al centro della stretta stanza, ideale per chi usi le altre funzioni del bagno solo di tanto in tanto. Una serie di luci artificiali regolabili si adatta allo stato d'animo dell'utente.

El estudio de Leonardo Anecca ha transformado un oscuro rincón de almacenaje en un lavabo acogedor y divertido. Una de las soluciones para aprovechar el espacio consiste en la instalación de una ducha justo en el centro de la estrecha habitación, solución óptima para quien use las restantes funciones del baño sólo ocasionalmente. Una serie de luces artificiales regulables se adaptan al estado de ánimo del usuario.

Le studio de Leonardo Anecca a transformé un coin sombre destiné au stockage en toilettes accueillantes et amusantes. Une des solutions pour profiter de l'espace était d'installer une douche en plein milieu de la pièce étroite, solution optimale pour qui utilise les fonctions restantes de la salle de bain seulement de façon occasionnelle. Une série de lumières artificielles réglables s'adapte à l'envie de l'utilisateur.

In de studio van Leonardo Anecca is een donkere opslaghoek omgetoverd in een aangename en leuke toiletruimte. Een van de grapjes die Anecca heeft bedacht om de ruimte te benutten is de douche in het midden van het krappe vertrek, een prima oplossing gezien het spaarzame gebruik van deze functie. Het regelbare kunstlicht kan worden afgestemd op het humeur van de gebruiker.

Architect: Leonardo Anecca
Photography: HappyLiving.dk
Location: Paris, France

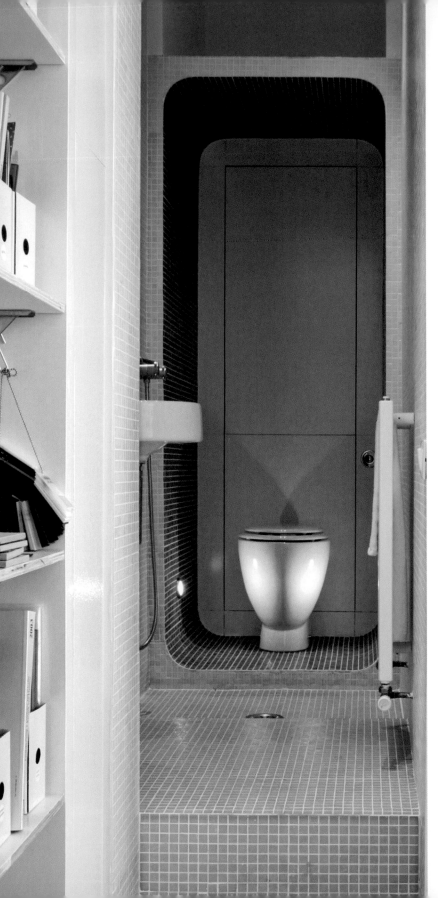

The bright red walls and interior of the cubicle containing the toilet are tiled with mosaics made by Bisazza. The lighting system was the responsibility of Inedit Paris.

Le pareti e l'interno del cubicolo che ospita la tazza del WC sono stati dipinti di rosso intenso e rivestiti con mosaici Bisazza. L'impianto di illuminazione è stato curato da Inedit Paris.

Las paredes y el interior del cubículo que alberga el inodoro, de un rojo intenso, están revestidas de mosaicos de Bisazza. El sistema de iluminación corre a cargo de Inedit Paris.

Les murs et l'intérieur des W.C., d'un rouge intense, sont recouverts de mosaïque de Bisazza. Le système d'éclairage est conçu par Inedit Paris.

De muren en het interieur van de wc-ruimte, waar de felrode pot staat, zijn bekleed met mozaïek van Bisazza. De verlichting is verzorgd door Inedit Paris.

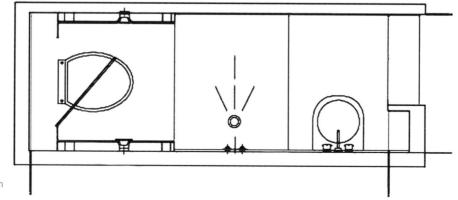

Floor plan

BULLRING
SHOPPING CENTER

The bathrooms in this shopping mall contain both cubicles separated by high partitions and private ones equipped with their own washbasins, to ensure greater privacy. Indirect lighting systems reduce the stress levels while photographic images create a soothing effect through a series of different spaces adapted to the needs of various groups of users.

I bagni di questo centro commerciale includono tazze WC separate da alti scomparti e cubicoli privati dotati di lavabo, al fine di garantire una maggiore intimità. Appositi sistemi di illuminazione indiretta riducono i livelli di stress, e varie immagini fotografiche percorrono una serie di spazi diversi, adattati alle esigenze dei vari gruppi di utenti, cercando di far svanire le inibizioni.

Los lavabos de este centro comercial incluyen inodoros separados por particiones altas, así como cubículos privados equipados con sus propios lavamanos para garantizar una mayor intimidad. Sistemas de iluminación indirecta reducen los niveles de estrés e imágenes fotográficas relajan a los inhibidos a lo largo de toda una serie de espacios distintos, adaptados a las necesidades de diferentes colectivos.

Les toilettes de ce centre commercial ont des W.C. divisés par de hautes séparations; il existe également des W.C. privatifs équipés de lavabos qui garantissent une plus grande intimité. Des systèmes d'éclairage indirect réduisent les niveaux de stress et des images photographiques relaxent les personnes inhibées tout au long d'une série de différents espaces adaptés aux besoins des divers utilisateurs.

De toiletpotten in dit winkelcentrum worden door hoge wanden van elkaar gescheiden. Elk toilet heeft zijn eigen wastafel wat het privacygevoel aanmerkelijk versterkt. Het indirecte licht en de fotobeelden hebben beide een stressverlagende uitwerking op het winkelende publiek.

Architect: Amalgam
Year: 2003
Photography: Phillip Vile
Location: Birmingham, UK

Areas specially designed for families include low toilet seats made for children, as well as folding chairs to provide greater comfort for breastfeeding mothers.

Alcuni spazi, pensati specialmente per le famiglie, includono tazze WC non molto alte, adatte ai bambini, così come sedie pieghevoli per un allattamento più comodo.

Espacios especialmente diseñados para las familias incluyen inodoros de menor altura para niños, así como asientos desplegables para un amamantamiento más cómodo.

Des espaces spécialement designés pour les familles proposent des W.C. plus petits pour les enfants, ainsi que des sièges pliables pour que les mamans puissent allaiter plus commodément.

In de aparte gezinsgedeelten bevinden zich speciale lage kinderwc-tjes en uitklapbare stoeltjes waarop moeders hun baby's de borst kunnen geven.

OFFICES BISAZZA

The architects designed an opulent, sumptuous bath-room with surfaces entirely covered with mosaics for the offices of Bisazza, the top-ranking producer of glass mosaics. The walls and ceiling alternate black pieces with fragments of white gold (24-carat strips of various sizes placed between two protective pieces of glass).

Per gli uffici della Bisazza, azienda leader nella pro-duzione di mosaici in vetro, gli architetti hanno dise-gnato un bagno sfarzoso e sontuoso dove la totalità delle superfici è rivestita da mosaici. Le pareti e il sof-fitto intercalano elementi neri con frammenti d'oro bianco, formati da lastre d'oro a 24 carati inserite tra due vetri di protezione, in pezzi di varie dimensioni.

Para estas oficinas de Bisazza, empresa líder en la producción de mosaicos de vidrio, los arquitectos di-señaron un baño opulento y suntuoso en que la totali-dad de las superficies está cubierta por mosaicos. Las paredes y el techo intercalan piezas negras con frag-mentos de oro blanco, constituidos por láminas de oro de 24 kilates puestas entre dos vidrios de protección, en piezas de varios tamaños.

Pour ces bureaux de Bisazza, entreprise leader dans la production de mosaïque en verre, les architectes ont designé une salle de bain opulente et somptueu-se dans laquelle la totalité des surfaces est recouverte par de la mosaïque. Les murs et le plafond intercalent des pièces noires avec des fragments d'or blanc, constitués par des lamelles d'or de 24 carats placées entre deux verres de protection, en pièces de diffé-rentes tailles.

Voor de kantoren van Bisazza, marktleider op het ge-bied van glazen mozaïeken, hebben de architecten een weelderige luxeuze toiletruimte ontworpen waar-in alle oppervlakken bedekte zijn met mozaïeken. In de wanden en het plafond zijn stukjes zwart en wit-goud van verschillende afmetingen verwerkt, gemaakt van 24-karaats goud, die geplaatst zijn tussen twee lagen veiligheidsglas.

Architect: Carlo Dal Bianco, Mauro Braggion
Photography: Alberto Ferrero
Location: Vicenza, Italy

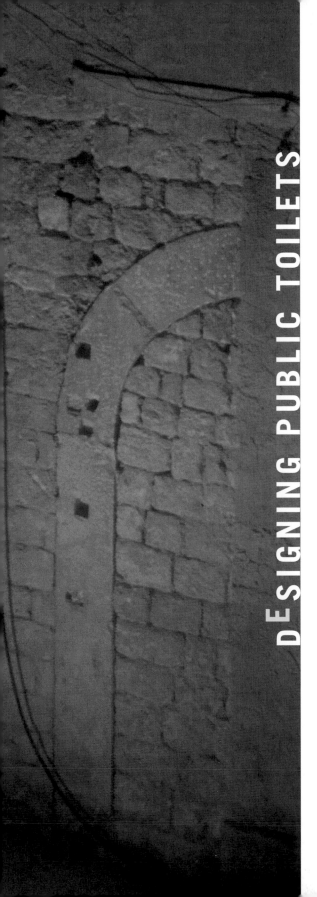

DESIGNING PUBLIC TOILETS

COMMUTING SPACES

The following selection of bathrooms at sites like railroad stations and airports, or on the street itself, reveals a growing concern with vandalism and delinquency in this type of public facility. Architects and designers go to great lengths to create safe, hygienic structures that are also visually attractive and inviting. Versatile materials and easy-to-clean surfaces are complemented by elegant, often minimalist exteriors that seek to blend into the urban landscape with the least possible impact.

La presente selezione rivela la preoccupazione sempre crescente di eliminare gli atti vandalici e la delinquenza nei servizi pubblici siti nelle stazioni ferroviarie, negli aeroporti, o direttamente in strada. Architetti e designer fanno del loro meglio per creare strutture igieniche e sicure che siano al contempo attraenti visivamente e che invitino al loro uso. Materiali versatili e superfici facili da pulire accompagnano esterni eleganti e frequentemente minimalisti che intendono integrarsi nel paesaggio urbano creando il minimo impatto possibile.

Sea en estaciones ferroviarias, en aeropuertos o en aseos situados en plena calle, la presente selección revela una creciente preocupación por acabar con el vandalismo y la delincuencia en este tipo de servicios públicos. Arquitectos y diseñadores se esfuerzan en crear estructuras higiénicas, seguras y visualmente atractivas, que inviten a su uso. Materiales versátiles y superficies de fácil limpieza se corresponden con exteriores elegantes y frecuentemente minimalistas, que buscan integrarse en el paisaje urbano con un mínimo impacto.

Que ce soit dans des gares ferroviaires, dans les aéroports ou dans des W.C. en pleine rue, la sélection proposée montre une préoccupation croissante pour en finir avec le vandalisme et la délinquance dans ce genre de services publics. Des architectes et des designers se sont à la fois efforcés de créer des structures hygiéniques et sûres mais aussi visuellement attrayantes pour inviter les personnes à les utiliser. Des matériaux évoluant avec le temps et des surfaces faciles à nettoyer correspondent à des extérieurs élégants et souvent minimalistes qui cherchent à intégrer le paysage urbain avec un impact minimum.

Of het nu gaat om stationsgebouwen, luchthavens of openbare toiletten op straat, in de volgende ontwerpen is vooral rekening gehouden met vandalisme- en misdaadpreventie. Architecten en ontwerpers doen hun uiterste best om sanitair te ontwikkelen waarbij hygiëne en veiligheid hand in hand gaan maar waarbij ook gedacht is aan het visuele aspect en de gebruiksvriendelijkheid. Flexibele materialen en makkelijk te reinigen oppervlakken zijn gecombineerd met elegante en veelal minimalistische ontwerpen die nauw aansluiten bij het stadslandschap.

DON'T MISS A SEC

This revolutionary project by the artist Monica Bonvicini was set up during the Art Basel 35 fair to investigate the reactions of visitors in the act of going to the bathroom. The module, comprising a stainless-steel toilet and washbasin, was inserted in a box of mirrors that reflected the outside world. The occupants inside are surrounded by a glass casing of startling transparency.

Questo rivoluzionario progetto dell'artista Monica Bonvicini è stato installato durante la fiera Art Basel 35 con l'obiettivo di studiare le reazioni della gente davanti alla necessità di andare in bagno. Il modulo, composto da una tazza WC e un lavabo realizzati in acciaio inossidabile, è contenuto in un parallelepipedo di specchi che riflette il mondo esterno, visibile agli occupanti, grazie alle pareti a specchio trasparenti.

Este revolucionario proyecto de la artista Monica Bonvicini se instaló durante la feria Art Basel 35 con el fin de investigar las reacciones de la gente frente al acto de ir al baño. El módulo, compuesto de un inodoro y un lavabo realizados en acero inoxidable, se introduce en una caja de espejos que refleja el mundo exterior. Los ocupantes, en el interior, están rodeados por un armazón de cristal de una transparencia chocante.

Ce projet révolutionnaire de l'artiste Monica Bonvicini a été créé pendant la foire Art Basel 35 afin de comprendre les réactions des gens lorsqu'ils doivent aller aux toilettes. Le module, composé d'un W.C. et d'un lavabo en acier inoxydable, a été introduit dans une caisse en verre qui reflète le monde extérieur. Les occupants, à l'intérieur, sont entourés d'une armature en verre d'une transparence choquante

Dit revolutionaire project van kunstenares Monica Bonvicini is neergezet tijdens Art Basel 35 met als doel om bezoekers te confronteren met hun privacygevoelens tijdens het toiletgebruik. De module, bestaande uit een wc en een wastafel van roestvrij staal, is ingebed in een spiegelruimte die de buitenwereld weerspiegelt. De toiletgebruiker wordt omringd door een glazen constructie die verbazingwekkend transparant is.

Architect: Monica Bonvicini
Year: 2003
Photography: c/o Galleria Emi Fontana, Milano
Location: Basel, Switzerland

Inside, the occupant uses the bathroom while observing the world around him or her; from the outside, the module looks like an opaque, sealed box that provides protection from curious onlookers.

All'interno, gli occupanti fanno uso del bagno mentre osservano, senza essere visti, ciò che avviene all'esterno. Da fuori, il modulo ha l'aspetto di una scatola opaca ed ermetica che protegge dagli sguardi curiosi dei passanti.

En el interior, el ocupante hace uso del baño mientras observa el mundo a su alrededor. Desde el exterior, el módulo tiene la apariencia de una caja opaca y hermética que protege de las miradas curiosas.

A l'intérieur, l'occupant utilise les toilettes pendant qu'il observe les gens tout autour. De l'extérieur, le module ressemble à une caisse opaque et hermétique qui protège des regards indiscrets des passants.

Hij kan zodoende zijn behoefte doen terwijl hij de wereld om zich heen bekijkt. Van buitenaf lijkt de module echter een ondoorzichtige, hermetisch afgesloten doos die je beschermt tegen nieuwsgierige blikken van buiten.

BRITOMART
TRANSPORT CENTER

The creation of a safe, visually attractive area was the primary objective of the refurbishment of this underground train station. This premise, along with the project's overall visual concept and identity, was also applied to the bathrooms. Consequently, resistant materials like stainless steel and concrete were combined with rich materials like mosaic, ceramics and glass.

Al momento di ridisegnare questa stazione ferroviaria sotterranea, l'obiettivo principale è stata la creazione di un'area sicura e visivamente attraente. Questa premessa, assieme al concetto dell'identità visuale dell'intero progetto, si applica anche alla concezione dei bagni. Per la loro realizzazione, sono stati utilizzati materiali resistenti come l'acciaio inossidabile e il calcestruzzo, mescolati con altri materiali ricchi come il mosaico, la ceramica e il vetro.

La creación de un área segura y visualmente atractiva fue el principal objetivo a la hora de rediseñar esta estación de tren subterránea. Esta premisa, junto con el concepto y la identidad visual de todo el proyecto, se aplica también a la concepción de los lavabos. Se empleó una paleta de materiales resistentes como el acero inoxidable y el cemento, mezclados con materiales ricos como el mosaico, la cerámica y el cristal.

La création d'une zone sûre et visuellement attrayante a été le principal objectif au moment de redesigner cette gare de train souterraine. Cet objectif, avec le concept et l'identité visuelle de tout le bâtiment, s'applique aussi au design des toilettes. On a employé une gamme de matériaux résistants comme l'acier inoxydable et le béton mélangés à des matériaux riches comme la mosaïque, la céramique et le verre.

De creatie van een veilig en visueel aantrekkelijk gebied was de belangrijkste doelstelling bij de herinrichting van dit metrostation. Deze doelstelling klinkt ook door in het ontwerp van de toiletten. Er zijn verschillende resistente materialen gebruikt zoals roestvrij staal en beton in combinatie met meer verfijnde stoffen als mozaïeken, keramiek en glas.

Architect: Jasmax with Mario Madayag Architecture
Photography: Elizabeth Goodall
Location: Auckland City, New Zealand

In order to maintain high levels of safety and hygiene, sensory taps and soap dispensers were installed, along with self-cleaning toilets. The system of green and blue lights gives each cubicle a distinctive character.

Al fine di mantenere i livelli di sicurezza ed igiene, e per evitare sprechi, sono stati usati rubinetti ed erogatori di sapone comandati da sensori a raggi infrarossi, e bagni autopulenti. Le tonalità verdi e azzurre dell'impianto di illuminazione imprimono un carattere distintivo a ogni servizio.

Para mantener los niveles de seguridad e higiene se incluyeron grifos y dispensadores de jabón activados por sensores, así como lavabos autolimpiantes. Sistemas de iluminación de tonalidades verdes y azules imprimen un carácter distintivo a cada servicio.

Pour maintenir les niveaux de sécurité et d'hygiène, des robinets et des dispensateurs sensoriels de savon ont été installés, tout comme des lavabos autonettoyants. Des systèmes d'éclairage dans les verts et les bleus attribuent un caractère différent à chaque W.C..

Ter waarborging van de veiligheid en hygiëne werden met sensoren uitgeruste kranen en zeepdispensers gemonteerd alsmede zelfreinigende toiletpotten. Lichtsystemen in groene en blauwe tinten geven een eigen karakter aan ieder toilet.

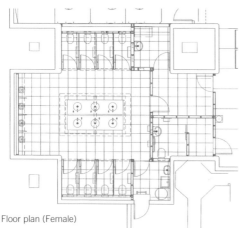

Floor plan (Female)

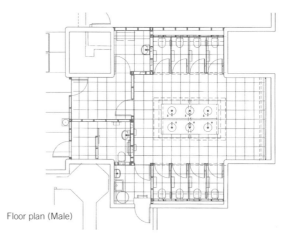

Floor plan (Male)

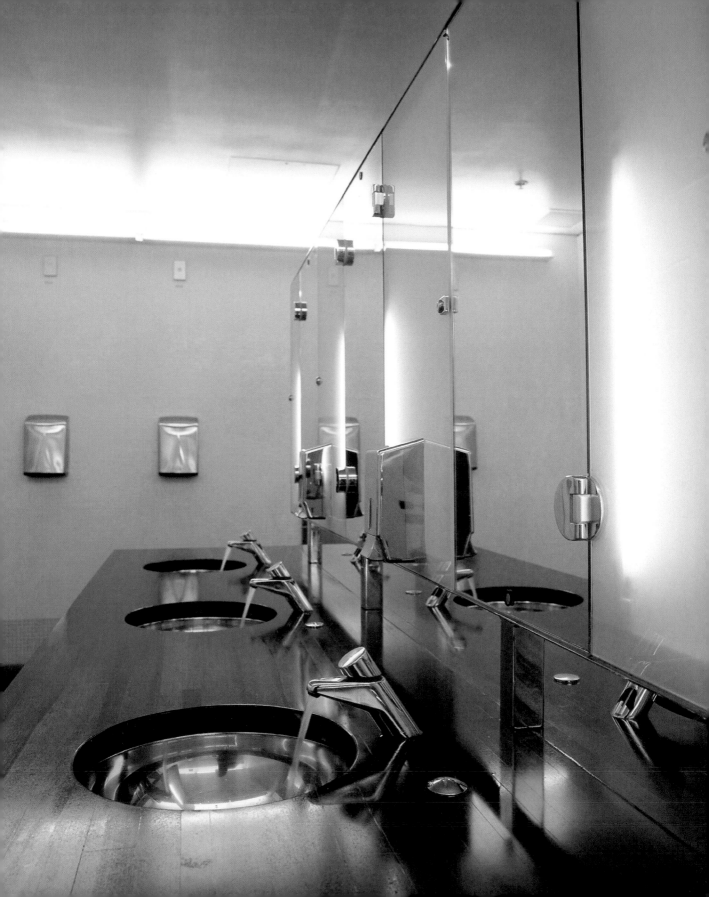

wEstBOURNE
GROVE PUBLIC LAVATORIES

The lively colors and the unusual shape of this building – rectangular at one end and triangular at the other – are a demonstration of how it is possible to imbue a public toilet with warmth, cheerfulness and modernity. The grooves on the façade break up the uniformity of the single color, while the round clock jutting from the wall balances the project and avoids any excessive preponderance of straight lines.

I colori vivaci e la forma peculiare di questo edificio, rettangolare a un'estremità e triangolare nell'altra, sono un esempio di come è possibile riempire di calore, allegria e modernità un bagno pubblico. Le scanalature della facciata spezzano l'uniformità della tinta unica e un orologio rotondo che sporge dalla parete equilibra il progetto ed ovvia all'eccessiva preponderanza della linea retta.

Los colores vivaces y la forma peculiar de este edificio, rectangular en un extremo y triangular en el otro, son una muestra de como es posible llenar un baño público de calidez, alegría y modernidad. Las estrías de la fachada rompen con la uniformidad del color único y un reloj redondo que sobresale de la pared equilibra el proyecto y evita la excesiva preponderancia de la línea recta.

Les couleurs vives et la forme particulière de ce bâtiment, rectangulaire d'un côté et triangulaire de l'autre, nous prouvent qu'il est possible de réaliser des toilettes publiques en leur donnant une note de chaleur, de joie et de modernité. Les stries de la façade cassent l'uniformité de couleur unique; une horloge ronde ressortant du mur équilibre le projet et évite la prépondérance excessive de la ligne droite.

De levendige kleuren en eigenaardige vorm van dit gebouw – rechthoekig aan een zijde en driehoekig aan de andere – tonen dat het mogelijk is om een openbaar toilet een warme, vrolijke en moderne uitstraling te geven. De groeven in de façade breken de uniformiteit van het kleurgebruik, voorkomen dat de rechte lijn de boventoon voert en brengen samen met de opvallende ronde klok evenwicht in het geheel.

Architect: CZWG
Photography: Chris Gascoigne/View
Location: London, Uk

The graphics on the entrance doors to the bathrooms play a very important role in the esthetic of the building and help give a contemporary look to the entire structure.

Le immagini presenti sulle porte di ingresso dei bagni svolgono un ruolo molto importante nell'estetica dell'edificio, e contribuiscono a dare a tutta la struttura un tocco di contemporaneità.

El grafismo, presente en las puertas de entrada de los baños, desempeña un papel muy importante en la estética del edificio y contribuye a proporcionar un diseño contemporáneo a toda la estructura.

Le graphisme, présent sur les portes d'entrée des toilettes, joue un rôle dans l'esthétique du bâtiment et contribue à donner un design contemporain à l'ensemble de la structure.

De grafische kunst op de deuren van de toiletten speelt een belangrijke rol in de esthetiek van het gebouw en zorgt voor een eigentijdse uitstraling.

PUBLIC TOILETS
IN SÃO PAULO

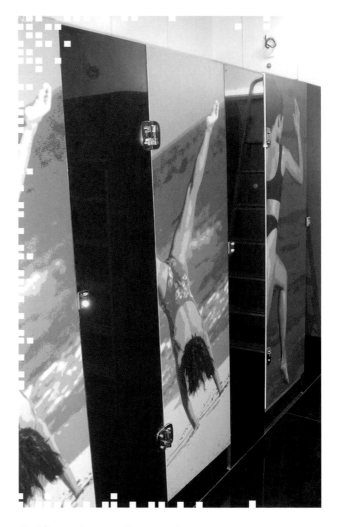

Severity and informality present a harmonious contrast in this showpiece of architecture and design. The black Marquina marble highlights the nakedness of the athletic bodies depicted on the doors to the cubicles. These daring visuals are not at odds with elegance, and the privacy of the bathroom does not negate the uninhibited dynamism of a stormy sea of waves.

Serietà ed informalità appaiono in contrasto armonico in questo singolare esempio di architettura e design. La nudità dei corpi atletici illustrati sulle porte dei bagni mette in risalto il marmo in nero Marquina. Chi l'ha detto che l'eleganza non va d'accordo con l'audacia? Persino l'atmosfera pacata e intima del bagno non rinuncia ad attivare, senza alcun pudore, un certo dinamismo in mezzo alle onde di un mare in tempesta.

Seriedad e informalidad contrastan armónicamente en esta muestra de arquitectura y diseño. El mármol negro de Marquina resalta sobre la desnudez de los cuerpos atléticos que adornan las puertas de los lavabos. La elegancia no está reñida con la osadía, y la intimidad reservada para el cuarto de baño no prescinde del dinamismo de olas sin pudor que agitan un mar en tempestad.

Dans cet exemple singulier d'architecture et de design, sérieux et non conventionnel forment un contraste harmonieux. Le marbre de couleur noire ressort avec la nudité des corps athlétiques dessinés sur les portes des toilettes. L'élégance n'est pas incompatible avec l'audace. Un certain dynamisme se ressent, sans aucune pudeur, malgré le calme et l'intimité réservés aux salles de bain, et permet de faire fonctionner le système sans se préoccuper des bruits.

Ernst en informaliteit vormen een harmonieus contrast in dit staaltje van design en architectuur. Het zwarte marmer benadrukt de naaktheid van de atletische lichamen die op de deuren van de toiletten zijn afgebeeld. De elegantie is niet in tegenspraak met de durf, en de intimiteit die hoort bij wc's vormt geen obstakel voor de onbeschaamde dynamiek die uit dit bruisende ontwerp spreekt.

Architect: Brunete Fraccaroli
Year: 2004
Photography: Tuca Reines
Location: São Paulo, Brazil

GONVILLE
PLACE PUBLIC CONVENIENCES

In 2002, the city of Cambridge held a competition to design new public toilets. The winning project was that of Freeland Rees Roberts Architects, whose main concern was to find a design suited to the prevention of ill-usage and vandalism. They created, for this purpose, an octogonal building with five prefabricated cubicles that open on to the exterior, to avoid enclosed spaces.

Nel 2002, la città di Cambridge ha indetto un concorso per la realizzazione dei nuovi bagni pubblici. Il progetto vincitore è stato quello dello studio Freeland Rees Roberts Architects: il design é stato concepito per ovviare a un uso improprio dei servizi e a eventuali atti di vandalismo. All'uopo, è stato creato un edificio a pianta ottagonale con cinque cubicoli prefabbricati e aperti all'esterno per evitare gli spazi chiusi.

En el 2002, la ciudad de Cambridge convocó un concurso para diseñar los nuevos servicios públicos. El proyecto ganador fue el de Freeland Rees Roberts Architects, cuya preocupación principal fue la de evitar el mal uso de los baños y el vandalismo a través de un diseño adecuado. A tal efecto crearon un edificio de planta octogonal con cinco cubículos prefabricados y abiertos al exterior para evitar los espacios cerrados.

En 2002, la ville de Cambridge a convoqué un concours pour designer les nouvelles toilettes publiques. Le projet gagnant, celui de Freeland Rees Roberts Architects, avait comme principale préoccupation d'éviter la mauvaise utilisation des toilettes et le vandalisme grâce à un design adéquat. Un bâtiment octogonal avec cinq compartiments préfabriqués a été créé à cet effet ; ils restent ouverts sur l'extérieur pour éviter les espaces fermés.

In 2002 schreef Cambridge een wedstrijd uit voor het ontwerp van de nieuwe openbare toiletten van de stad. Winnaar Freeland Rees Roberts Architects had als insteek dat misbruik en vandalisme voorkomen kunnen worden via een adequaat ontwerp. Daartoe werd een achthoekig gebouw neergezet met vijf pregefabriceerde kamertjes die in open verbinding staan met de buitenwereld om een gesloten ruimte te vermijden.

Architect: Freeland Rees Roberts Architects
Year: 2004
Photography: Peter Cook
Location: Cambridge, UK

The red, orange and yellow walls stand out against the park, while a series of cathode lamps that gradually change color light up the building at night, making it seem like a carousel in a fairground.

Le pareti di color rosso, arancione e giallo ricordano quelle di un bosco autunnale. Di sera, una serie di luci catodiche che cambiano gradualmente di colore illumina l'edificio facendolo somigliare alla giostra di un luna park.

Las paredes rojas, naranjas y amarillas refuerzan los motivos del parque, mientras que una serie de luces catódicas que cambian gradualmente de coloR iluminan el edificio de noche y hacen que se parezca a un carrusel de un parque de atracciones.

Les murs rouges, oranges et jaunes renforcent les motifs du parc, tandis qu'une série de lumières cathodiques qui changent graduellement de couleur, illuminent le soir le bâtiment et lui confèrent un air de carrousel de parc d'attractions.

De rode, oranje en gele wanden zijn in harmonie met de parkachtige omgeving terwijl een serie lampen, die langzaam van kleur veranderen, het gebouw 's avonds verlichten, waardoor het een draaimolen lijkt in een attractiepark.

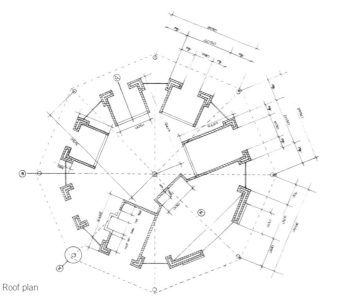

Roof plan

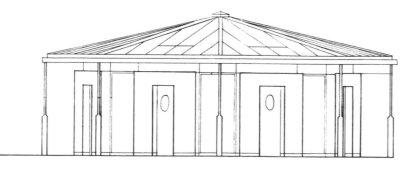

Elevation

AIR CANADA
MAPLE LEAF LOUNGE

Air Canada wanted to create spacious, tranquil and elegant bathrooms incorporating private showers that would be attractive to a wide range of users in its new VIP zone in Toronto airport. The porcelain floors are complemented by walls tiled with mosaics that add texture to the surfaces and create an austere but attractive decoration.

Per il nuovo spazio VIP della compagnia aerea Air Canada, situato all'interno dell'aeroporto di Toronto, sono stati creati dei bagni spaziosi, rilassanti ed eleganti, attraenti per un vasto gruppo di utenti e dotati di docce private. I pavimenti di porcellana si completano con pareti rivestite di mosaico che aggiungono una speciale trama alle superfici e danno luogo a una decorazione sobria ma allo stesso tempo seducente.

Para el nuevo espacio VIP de la compañía aérea Air Canada, ubicado en el aeropuerto de Toronto, se quiso crear unos lavabos espaciosos, serenos y elegantes que resultaran atractivos para un amplio grupo de usuarios y que incorporaran duchas privadas. Los suelos de porcelana se complementan con paredes revestidas de mosaico, que añaden textura a las superficies y dan lugar a una decoración sobria y a la vez atractiva.

Pour le nouvel espace VIP de la compagnie aérienne Air Canada, situé dans l'aéroport de Toronto, on a voulu créer des toilettes spacieuses, sereines et élégantes, attrayantes pour un grand groupe d'utilisateurs et qui seront équipées de douches privées. Les sols en porcelaine s'harmonisent aux murs recouverts de mosaïque et donnent de la texture aux surfaces. L'ensemble est décoré d'une manière sobre et agréable.

Voor de nieuwe viproom van luchtvaartmaatschappij Air Canada op de luchthaven van Toronto wilde men ruim, sereen en elegant sanitair dat aantrekkelijk is voor een grote groep gebruikers en waar ook gedoucht kan worden. De porseleinen vloeren worden gecompleteerd met de met mozaïek beklede wanden die textuur geven aan de oppervlakken en zorgen voor een sobere en tegelijkertijd aantrekkelijke aankleding.

Architect: II by IV Design Associates
Year: 2004
Photography: David Whittaker
Location: Toronto, Canada

KROS URINAL

This urinal, permanently installed in the open air, seeks to curb urination in the street. The unit is only open at night – when this problem is most acute – and it stays closed during the day to prevent vandalism. The materials used can be cleaned easily and the elegant, essential design is intended to cause a minimal impact on the surrounding architecture.

Questo orinatoio, permanentemente installato all'aria aperta, intende mettere un freno all'orinazione pubblica per strada. L'unità, realizzata con materiali che ne consentono una facile pulizia, viene aperta soltanto di sera, momento in cui si accusa di più questo problema, e rimane chiusa durante la giornata onde evitare che subisca atti di vandalismo. In quanto al design, si sono scelte linee eleganti e minimaliste, con un impatto minimo sull'architettura circostante.

Permanentemente instalado al aire libre, este urinario pretende controlar la micción callejera. La unidad se abre sólo durante la noche, momento en que más se acusa este problema, y permanece cerrado durante el día a fin de prevenir el vandalismo. Los materiales utilizados permiten una fácil limpieza y el diseño, elegante y minimalista, está pensado para causar un mínimo impacto sobre la arquitectura que lo rodea.

Installé de façon permanente à l'air libre, cet urinoir a pour but d'empêcher les gens d'uriner dans la rue. L'unité est ouverte seulement la nuit, moment le plus propice à ce genre de problème, et reste fermé pendant la journée afin de prévenir le vandalisme. Les matériaux utilisés permettent un nettoyage facile et le design, élégant et minimaliste, est pensé pour causer un minimum d'impact sur l'architecture environnante.

Dit urinoir moet wildplassers op andere gedachten brengen. Het is alleen 's avonds geopend, wanneer wilplassers het meest actief zijn. Overdag blijft de eenheid gesloten om vandalisme te voorkomen. De gebruikte materialen zijn makkelijk te reinigen en het elegante en minimalistische design is zo bedacht dat het zo weinig mogelijk impact heeft op de omgeving.

Architect: Lacock Gullam/Oblique Workshops
Year: 2001
Photography: Speller Milner Design
Location: London, UK

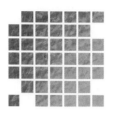

PUBLIC TOILETS IN THE FOREST

With its gentle forms made of aged steel, this small bathroom pavilion in a wood appears more like an elegant sculpture than a building. Its seamless, luminous forms contain changing rooms, showers, bathrooms and a refreshment stand. The pavilion undulates slightly in order to avoid any possible floods, while the daylight filters through the perforated steel plates.

Questo piccolo padiglione, installato in mezzo a un bosco, somiglia più a un'elegante scultura che a un edificio. Nei suoi volumi di acciaio invecchiato, leggeri e luminosi, c'è spazio per spogliatoi, docce, lavabi e un chiosco di bibite. Il padiglione appare leggermente ondulato al fine di evitare possibili inondazioni; la luce solare filtra attraverso le lastre di acciaio perforato.

Con sus suaves volúmenes de acero envejecido, este diminuto pabellón de baño dentro del bosque se parece más a una elegante escultura que a un edificio. Sus volúmenes luminosos y sin costuras dan cabida a vestuarios, duchas, lavabos y a un quiosco de bebidas. El pabellón aparece ligeramente ondulado a fin de evitar posibles inundaciones, mientras la luz del día se filtra a través de las planchas de acero perforado.

Avec ses doux volumes en acier vieilli, ce petit pavillon hébergeant des toilettes, à l'intérieur d'un bois, ressemble plus à une élégante sculpture qu'à un bâtiment. Ses volumes lumineux proposent des vestiaires, des douches, des lavabos et un kiosque à boissons. Le pavillon a une forme légèrement ondulée afin d'éviter les risques d'inondation. La lumière du jour se filtre à travers les planches d'acier perforé.

Met zijn prachtige, zachte staalconstructies lijkt dit piepkleine paviljoen in het bos eerder een elegante sculptuur dan een gebouw. Behalve een kleedruimte, douches en toiletten, bevat dit paviljoen ook nog een kiosk waar je drankjes kunt krijgen. Het gebouw is lichtglooiend om mogelijke overstromingen te voorkomen. Het daglicht wordt gefilterd doorgelaten door de geperforeerde staalconstructies.

Architect: Aranda Pigem Vilalta Arquitectes
Year: 1998
Photography: Jordi Miralles
Location: Olot, Spain

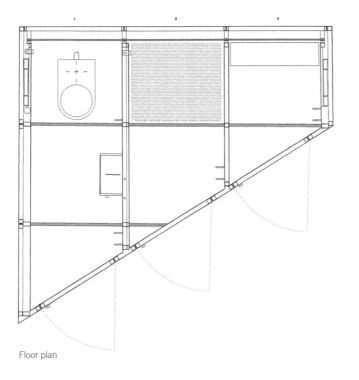

Floor plan

A slight curve in the contours and the smooth metallic surfaces endow the project with a delicate imbalance and a distinctive expressiveness.

Una leggera curva nella pianta e le morbide superfici metalliche imprimono al progetto un delicato squilibrio e un carattere peculiare, che lo dotano di espressività.

Una ligera curva en el plano y las suaves superficies metálicas imprimen al proyecto un delicado desequilibrio y un carácter peculiar que lo dotan de expresividad.

Une courbe légère et des surfaces métalliques douces déséquilibrent délicatement le bâtiment tout en le dotant d'une expressivité propre.

Een kleine buiging in het ontwerp en de gladde metalen oppervlakken zorgen voor een lichte verstoring van het evenwicht, wat bijdraagt aan het bijzondere en expressieve karakter van dit project.

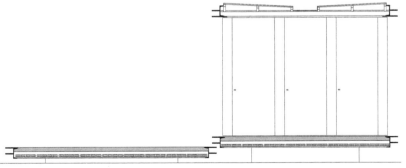

Section

1² APOSTLES

Vernacular architecture plays a very important role in this building, drawn up by the prize-winning Australian architect Greg Burgess. The complex includes a tourist information center and an area with public bathrooms. It takes advantage of traditional construction techniques, fused with an innovative use of new materials, particularly marked by an outstanding presence of steel and glass.

L'architettura nativa ha una presenza molto importante in questo edificio, progettato dal premiato architetto australiano Greg Burgess. Il complesso, che include un centro di informazioni turistiche e un'area con i bagni pubblici, presenta alcune tecniche costruttive tradizionali che si fondono con un impiego innovativo di nuovi materiali, tra cui spicca l'uso eccezionale dell'acciaio e del vetro.

La arquitectura autóctona tiene una presencia muy importante en este edificio, proyectado por el premiado arquitecto australiano Greg Burgess. El complejo incluye un centro de información turística y un área de baños públicos y presenta técnicas constructivas tradicionales que se fusionan con un uso innovador de nuevos materiales, entre los cuales destaca el empleo certero del acero y del cristal.

L'architecture du lieu est très présente dans ce bâtiment conçu par l'architecte australien primé Greg Burgess. Le complexe comprend un centre d'informations touristiques et un espace pour les toilettes publiques. Il présente des techniques de construction traditionnelle qui fusionnent avec une utilisation novatrice de nouveaux matériaux, parmi lesquels l'acier et le verre, employés à juste titre.

De inheemse architectuur speelt een belangrijke rol in dit gebouw dat is ontworpen door de bekroonde Australische architect Greg Burgess. Het complex omvat een toeristisch informatiecentrum en een toiletgedeelte. Traditionele bouwtechnieken worden hierbij gecombineerd met het innovatieve gebruik van nieuwe materialen, waarbij de staal- en glasconstructies het meest in het oog springen.

Architect: Greg Burgess
Photography: Meinphoto
Location: Campbell National Park, Australia

Local traditions blend with contemporary trends in this project replete with ideas about the concept of fusion, which is omnipresent in nature.

La tradizione indigena si associa alle tendenze contemporanee in questo progetto ricco di messaggi sulla nozione di fusione, molto presente nella natura.

La tradición indígena se conjuga con tendencias contemporáneas en este proyecto rico en mensajes sobre la noción de fusión, tan presente en la naturaleza.

Dans ce projet riche en messages sur la notion de fusion, si présente dans la nature, la tradition autochtone se conjugue aux tendances contemporaines.

De inheemse traditie versmelt in dit bijzondere project met moderne kennis, waardoor het in harmonie is met de omgeving.

PUBLIC RESTROOMS
AT KADIKOY PARK

The cities of Anatolia have a long tradition regarding sanitation services. This project was inspired by a desire to reassess the design of public toilets and achieve a building that was visually attractive as well as safe and clean. For this reason, the interior used a range of cheap, resistant materials that are easy to maintain, such as concrete and stainless steel.

Le città dell'Anatolia vantano una lunga tradizione per quanto riguarda i servizi sanitari. Questo progetto parte dalla volontà di ridisegnare i servizi pubblici dando loro un volto nuovo e creando una costruzione che sia bella da vedere ma anche pulita e sicura. Per questo motivo, per gli interni di questa unità sono stati adoperati materiali economici, resistenti e dalla facile manutenzione, come il cemento o l'acciaio inossidabile.

Las ciudades de Anatolia cuentan con una larga tradición en cuanto a servicios sanitarios se refiere. Este proyecto parte de la voluntad de replantear el diseño de los servicios públicos para lograr una construcción visualmente atractiva a la par que segura y limpia. De ahí que en el interior se haya empleado una paleta de materiales económicos, resistentes y de fácil mantenimiento como el cemento o el acero inoxidable.

Les villes d'Anatolie ont une longue tradition lorsqu'il s'agit de services sanitaires. Ce projet part de la volonté de repenser le design des services publics pour réaliser des constructions visuellement attrayantes mais aussi sûres et propres. On a ainsi utilisé pour l'intérieur une gamme de matériaux économiques, résistants et d'entretien facile comme le béton ou l'acier inoxydable.

De steden van Anatolië kunnen bogen op een eeuwenoude traditie op sanitair gebied. In het Kadikoy Park is getracht om een geheel nieuwe invulling te geven aan het ontwerp van sanitair waarbij een constructie tot stand is gekomen die visueel aantrekkelijk en tegelijkertijd veilig en schoon is. Daarom zijn in het interieur vooral goedkope, resistente en makkelijk te onderhouden materialen gebruikt zoals beton en roestvrij staal.

Architect: GAD Architecture
Year: 1997
Photography: GAD Architecture
Location: Istanbul, Turkey

A narrow window in the roof and the glass entrance doors allow sunlight to enter this underground bathroom.

La luce naturale penetra in questo bagno sotterraneo attraverso una stretta finestra posta nel soffitto e le porte di ingresso realizzate in vetro.

Una estrecha ventana situada en el techo y puertas de entrada realizadas en cristal proveen de luz natural este lavabo subterráneo.

D'étroites fenêtres en verre situées au plafond et sur les portes d'entrée fournissent la lumière naturelle à ce lavabo en sous-sol.

Een klein raam in het dak en glazen deuren zorgen voor natuurlijk licht in deze ondergrondse toiletruimte.

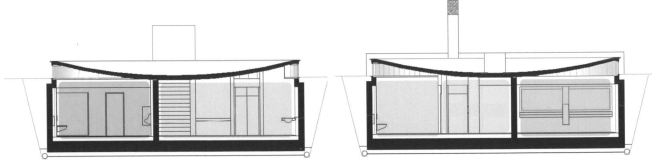

Section

DIA^N^A, PRINCESS OF WALES MEMORIAL PLAYGROUND

The design of the lavatories in this playground stirs the interest of children of all ages and backgrounds. Its bright colors and lively illustrations on the doors are inspired by Peter Pan, which is a recurring theme throughout the playground. A skylight situated above a two-washbasin module impregnates the space with natural light and bestows a sense of expansiveness and luminosity on the project.

Le avventure di Peter Pan sono il motivo di ispirazione che ricorre in tutti gli ambienti di questo parco infantile, compresi i bagni: il design, pieno di colori e con illustrazioni animate sulle porte, non smette di attirare l'attenzione di molti bambini, di età e provenienza diverse. Il lucernario posto al di sopra del modulo a due lavabi diffonde la luce naturale, ampliando la sensazione di luminosità e di respiro.

El diseño de los lavabos de este parque infantil atrae a niños de todas las edades y provenencias. Con un fuerte colorido y animadas ilustraciones en las puertas, debe su inspiración al libro de Peter Pan, tema recurrente en todos los ámbitos del parque. Un tragaluz situado sobre un módulo de dos lavamanos impregna el espacio de luz natural y otorga amplitud y luminosidad al proyecto.

Le design des toilettes de ce jardin d'enfants attire des enfants de tout âge et de toutes les nations. Avec des couleurs dominantes et des illustrations très gaies sur les portes, il doit son inspiration au livre de Peter Pan, thème présent dans tous les domaines du jardin. Une lucarne située au-dessus de deux lavabos imprègne l'espace de lumière naturelle et donne de l'amplitude et de la luminosité.

Het ontwerp van de toiletten in deze speeltuin heeft een grote aantrekkingskracht op kinderen van alle leeftijden en pluimage. Het felle kleurgebruik en de levendige illustraties op de deuren zijn geïnspireerd op Peter Pan, een thema dat ook in de rest van het park terugkeert.

Architect: Jestico + Whiles
Photography: James Morris
Location: London, UK

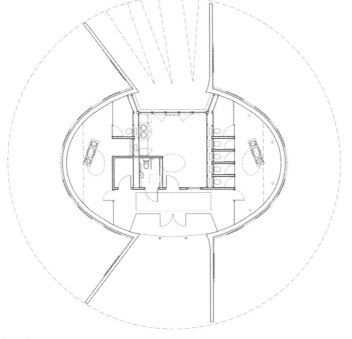

Floor plan

A circular skylight endows this project with natural light, giving it luminosity and spaciousness that contrast with the sealed appearance of its exterior.

Un lucernario situato su un modulo con due lavabi impregna lo spazio di luce naturale, conferendo ampiezza e luminosità a tutto il progetto.

Un tragaluz circular proporciona luz natural a este proyecto, dotándolo de una diafanidad que contrasta con la apariencia hermética de su exterior.

Une lucarne circulaire laisse entrer la lumière naturelle dans ce lieu tout en le dotant d'une translucidité qui contraste avec l'aspect hermétique de son extérieur.

Een lichtkoepel boven een van de wasbakken zorgt voor voldoende licht en maakt de ruimte minder klein en hermetisch dan je van buiten zou verwachten.

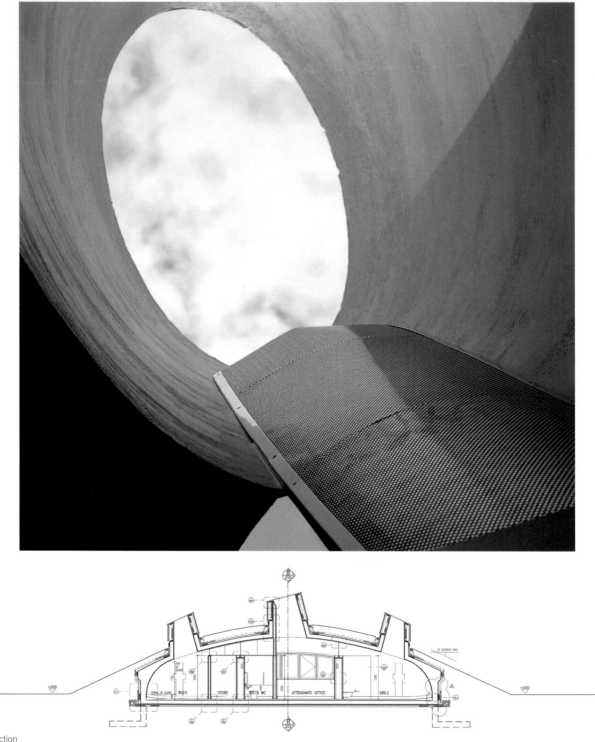

Section

T^OILET IN SMOLMARK

One alternative to the design of a bathroom suitably equipped to mask sounds and smells is its installation in a position where users do not need to concern themselves about the presence of other people. This lavatory is so isolated that it not only provides a user with total intimacy, but also allows him, or her, to leave the door open and enjoy the natural surroundings.

Per ovviare a ogni imbarazzo, un'alternativa possibile è quella di installare l'unità sanitaria in posti in cui l'utente non debba preoccuparsi della presenza o meno di altre persone. Il presente bagno si trova talmente isolato, che l'utente non solo può usufruire di una privacy assoluta, ma può addirittura lasciare la porta aperta, se lo desidera, e godersi il paesaggio.

Una alternativa al diseño de un lavabo adecuadamente equipado para enmascarar sonidos y olores reside en ubicar la instalación en algún emplazamiento donde el usuario no necesite preocuparse por la presencia de otras personas. El presente lavabo se encuentra tan aislado que su lejanía permite no sólo disponer de una absoluta intimidad, sino dejar la puerta abierta para poder disfrutar de la naturaleza que lo rodea.

Une solution alternative pour camoufler les bruits et les odeurs réside à l'installer dans un endroit où l'utilisateur n'a pas besoin de se préoccuper de la présence d'autres personnes. Les toilettes présentées se trouvent si éloignées qu'elles permettent non seulement de disposer d'une intimité absolue, mais aussi de laisser la porte ouverte pour pouvoir apprécier la nature qui les entoure.

Het alternatief voor een toiletdesign gericht op het maskeren van geluiden en geuren is de plaatsing van een wc op een plaats waar de gebruiker zich niet hoeft te bekommeren om de aanwezigheid van anderen. Deze wc ligt zo geïsoleerd dat de bezoeker verzekerd is van intimiteit en de deur eventueel gewoon open kan laten staan om te genieten van de natuur om zich heen.

Architect: 24H Architecture
Year: 2004
Photography: James Silverman
Location: Smolmark, Sweden

While seated on the toilet, the user becomes one with the surrounding landscape – a wood with a stream – that can be glimpsed through a slit.

Seduto sulla tazza del WC, l'utente si trova immerso negli elementi naturali che attorniano l'unità – il bosco e un ruscello – visibili attraverso una fessura.

Sentado en el inodoro, el usuario se halla inmerso en el paisaje que lo circunda – el bosque y un arroyo – que se divisan a través de una rendija.

Assis sur les W.C., l'utilisateur se trouve immergé dans le paysage environnant – le bois et un ruisseau – qui se voit à travers une fente.

Zittend op de pot word je omringd door de natuur – het bos en een beekje – die je met dichte deur ook via een spleet kunt zien.

DA**N**FO URINAL

Drug abuse and vandalism in London made it necessary to find safe, attractive alternatives capable of absorbing the flow of people passing through the West End. The industrial designers Lacock Gullam joined forces with the Swedish manufacturer Danfo to create this elegant, metal urinal that remains closed throughout the day and opens its wings after nightfall to receive up to 100 gallons of urine.

A Londra, l'abuso di droghe e i frequenti atti di vandalismo hanno reso necessarie delle alternative sicure e attraenti ai tradizionali bagni pubblici, come è accaduto nella frequentatissima zona del West End. Dalla collaborazione dei designer industriali Lacock Gullam con la ditta svedese Danfo, leader nella produzione di toilette, è nato questo originale ed elegante orinatoio metallico, che rimane chiuso durante il giorno e apre le sue porte al tramonto per raccogliere fino a 360 litri di urina.

En Londres, el abuso de drogas y el vandalismo hacía necesarias alternativas seguras y atrayentes que fueran capaces de absorber el flujo de gente que acude al West End. Los diseñadores industriales Lacock Gullam han colaborado con el fabricante sueco Danfo para crear este urinario metálico y elegante, que permanece cerrado durante el día y abre sus alas después del anochecer para recoger hasta 360 litros de orina.

A Londres, l'abus de drogues et le vandalisme rendaient nécessaires des alternatives sûres et attirantes capables d'absorber le flux de gens qui arrive dans le West End. Les designers industriels Lacock Gullam ont collaboré avec le fabricant suédois Danfo pour créer cet urinoir métallique et élégant qui reste fermé pendant la journée et ouvre lorsque la nuit tombe pour recueillir 360 litres d'urine.

In Londen dwongen druggebruik en vandalisme architecten ertoe op zoek te gaan naar veilige en aantrekkelijke alternatieven om de stroom mensen die West End bezoekt op te vangen. De industrieel ontwerpers van Lacock Gullam hebben in samenwerking met de Zweedse fabrikant Danfo deze metalen urinoir ontwikkeld die overdag dicht is en 's avonds zijn deuren opent om meer dan 360 liter urine te verwerken.

Architect: Lacock Gullam/Oblique Workshops
Year: 2002
Photography: Speller Milner Design
Location: London, UK

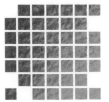 SCHIPHOL AIRPORT AMSTERDAM

The first and last impressions are the ones that stay in the mind, and this is demonstrated by the public bathrooms in Amsterdam airport, which synthetize the image of this country by means of the large images covering the walls and accessories. Tulips, windmills and sunflowers adorn what was once a stark, unappealing bathroom in an attempt to convert it into an unusual visual experience.

La prima e l'ultima impressione sono quelle che valgono e che rimangono impresse, e lo dimostrano i bagni pubblici dell'aeroporto di Amsterdam; le loro pareti e gli accessori sono rivestiti da diverse fotografie di grandi dimensioni che sintetizzano l'immagine di questo paese. Tulipani, mulini e campi di girasoli decorano questo spazio con l'intenzione di convertire un bagno anteriormente nudo e privo di attrattive, in un'esperienza visiva davvero sorprendente.

La primera y la última impresión son las que prevalecen, y así lo demuestran los baños públicos del aeropuerto de Amsterdam, que sintetizan la imagen de este país por medio de imágenes de grandes dimensiones que recubren paredes y accesorios. Tulipanes, molinos y campos de girasoles decoran este espacio en una voluntad de convertir un baño desnudo y desprovisto de atractivos en una experiencia visual sorprendente.

La première et la dernière impression sont celles qui prévalent. Les toilettes publiques de l'aéroport d'Amsterdam en sont l'exemple ; elles synthétisent l'image de ce pays grâce à des images de grandes dimensions qui recouvrent les murs et les accessoires. Des tulipes, des moulins et des champs de tournesols décorent cet espace et ont transformé ces toilettes, qui auparavant étaient nues et dépourvues de charme, en une expérience visuelle surprenante.

De eerste en laatste indruk blijven hangen, zo moeten de ontwerpers van deze toiletten op Schiphol hebben gedacht. De muren en accessoires van deze toiletten zijn versierd met afbeeldingen van de belangrijkste toeristische trekpleisters. Tulpen, molens en velden met zonnebloemen zorgen ervoor dat de eerst zo saaie toiletruimtes een verrassend visueel experiment zijn geworden.

Architect: Pilots Product Design
Year: 2003
Photography: Jop Timmers
Location: Amsterdam, the Netherlands

Opening the doors of this bathroom means stepping into a typically Dutch landscape, thanks to the array of images decorating the room and setting off an otherwise completely white space.

Aprire le porte di questo bagno significa addentrarsi nel tipico paesaggio olandese, le cui molteplici immagini decorano i vari ambienti e spiccano in uno spazio completamente bianco.

Abrir las puertas de este baño supone adentrarse en un paisaje típicamente holandés gracias a las múltiples imágenes que decoran la estancia y sobresalen en un espacio, por lo demás, completamente blanco.

Ouvrir les portes de ces toilettes veut dire pénétrer dans un paysage typiquement hollandais grâce aux nombreuses images qui décorent la pièce et se détachent dans un espace totalement blanc.

Als je de deur van de wc opentrekt, beland je in een typisch Hollands landschap dankzij de vele beelden die zijn aangebracht in de verder geheel witte ruimte.

WC P⁰DS
AT STRATFORD MARKET DEPOT

This transportable cubicle, originally designed for Stratford Market station, constitutes a veritable innovation in the design of public lavatories due to its efficient exploitation of space. It focuses on practical aspects (without forsaking elegant design): easy cleaning, ergonomic lines and the use of stainless steel, which is consistent, long-lasting and resists acts of vandalism.

Progettato originariamente per la stazione di Stratford Market, questa toilette mobile rappresenta una vera e propria novità nel design dei bagni pubblici, soprattutto per il modo efficace in cui sfrutta lo spazio a disposizione, senza comunque trascurare l'eleganza. Il cubicolo, facile da trasportare e da pulire, presenta linee ergonomiche ed è stato fabbricato in acciaio inossidabile, un materiale saldo e durevole, e che resiste bene agli atti vandalici.

Originalmente diseñado para la estación de Stratford Market, este cubículo transportable representa una auténtica innovación en el diseño de lavabos públicos por su eficaz aprovechamiento del espacio. Sin descuidar un diseño elegante, se centra sobre todo en los aspectos prácticos: fácil limpieza, líneas ergonómicas y fabricación en acero inoxidable, un material consistente, duradero y que resiste bien a los actos de vandalismo.

Originalement designé pour la gare de Stratford Market, ces W.C. transportables représentent une véritable innovation dans le design des toilettes publiques car ils tirent un profit maximal de l'espace. Sans laisser pour compte un design élégant, ils se concentrent surtout sur les aspects pratiques : nettoyage facile, lignes ergonomiques, fabrication en acier inoxydable, un matériau solide, durable et qui résiste bien aux actes de vandalisme.

Oorspronkelijk ontworpen voor het station van Stratford Market, is dit verplaatsbare toilet een echte innovatie op het gebied van openbare toiletten vanwege de efficiënte manier waarmee er met de ruimte wordt omgesprongen. Zonder de elegantie uit het oog te verliezen, richt dit ontwerp zich vooral op praktische zaken: makkelijke reiniging, ergonomische belijning en gebruik van roestvrij staal, een consistent en duurzaam materiaal dat bestand is tegen vandalisme.

Architect: Wilkinson Eyre Architects
Photography: Wilkinson Eyre Architects, Dennis Gilbert/View, Amé-EURO
Location: London, UK

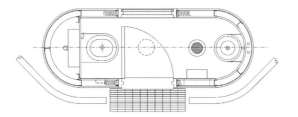

Floor plan

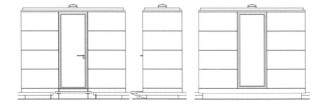

Elevation

The chromatic uniformity gives this bathroom a modern look that reinforces the functional concept, aimed at facilitating maintenance and discouraging vandalism.

L'uniformità cromatica conferisce a questo bagno un aspetto moderno, che ben si coniuga con la sua funzionalità e facilità di manutenzione.

La uniformidad cromática confiere a este baño una apariencia de modernidad que se conjuga con una concepción funcional, destinada a facilitar el mantenimiento y disuadir el vandalismo.

L'uniformité chromatique confère à ces toilettes une apparence moderne qui se conjugue à leur fonctionnalité, destinée à faciliter l'entretien et à dissuader les vandales.

De eenheid van kleur geeft deze wc een modern uiterlijk, wat een belangrijke aanvulling is op de eerder genoemde functionele aspecten.

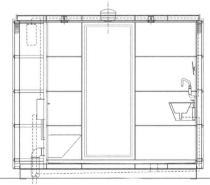

Section

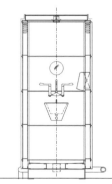

PUBLIC TOILETS
AT THE PORT OF DUBROVNIK

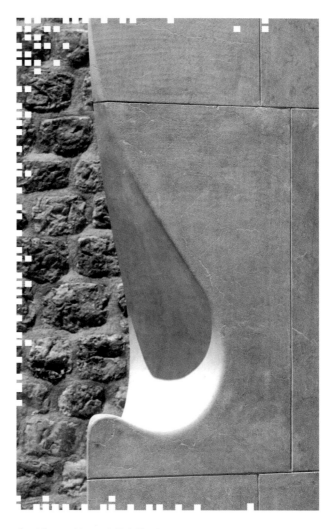

In the old port of Dubrovnik, just behind the medieval walls, lies this narrow building measuring 5 x 41 ft. The architect designed a structure with an elongated profile that would fit into this recently created passageway. Latrines, doors and stainless-steel washbasins situated in niches complete the ensemble, bounded by concrete exterior walls that contrast with the black stone inside.

Nel vecchio Porto di Dubrovnik, proprio dietro le antiche mura medievali, si trova questo stretto edificio, di 1,70 x 12,50 m. L'architetto ha progettato una struttura in modo che il suo profilo allungato si adattasse a questo andito creato di recente. Il complesso è formato da orinatoi, porte e lavabi di acciaio inossidabile, posti in appositi incavi; le pareti esterne di cemento contrastano con la pietra nera dell'interno.

En el antiguo Puerto de Dubrovnik, justo detrás de las antiguas murallas medievales, se encuentra este volumen estrecho de 1,70 x 12,50 m. El arquitecto diseñó una estructura cuyo perfil alargado se adaptara a este pasadizo recién creado. Letrinas, puertas y lavamanos de acero inoxidable situados en nichos completan el conjunto, con paredes exteriores de cemento que contrastan con la piedra negra del interior.

Dans le vieux port de Dubrovnik, juste derrière les anciennes murailles médiévales, se trouve ce bâtiment étroit de 1,70 x 12,50 m. L'architecte a designé une structure dont le profil allongé s'adapte à ce passage récemment créé. Des latrines, des portes et des lavabos en acier inoxydable situés dans des niches complètent l'ensemble, avec des murs externes fabriqués en béton qui contrastent avec la pierre noire de l'intérieur.

In de oude haven van Dubrovnik, net achter de middeleeuwse stadsmuren, bevindt zich dit smalle gebouwtje van 1,70 x 12,50 m. De architect heeft in zijn ontwerp rekening gehouden met de langgerektheid. De latrines, deuren en wasbakken van roestvrij staal zijn in nissen geplaatst.

Architect: Nenad Fabijanic
Photography: Nenad Fabijanic
Year: 2002
Location: Dubrovnik, Croatia

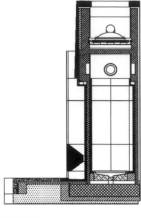

Section

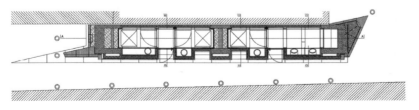

Floor plan

The interior, built with modern, industrial materials, contrasts with the city walls around this public bathroom.

L'interno, realizzato in materiali moderni e industriali, contrasta con le mura che circondano questo bagno pubblico.

El interior, realizado en materiales modernos e industriales, contrasta con las murallas que rodean este baño público.

L'intérieur, réalisé avec des matériaux modernes et industriels contraste avec les murailles qui entourent ces toilettes publiques.

De betonnen buitenmuren contrasteren met de zwarte steensoort die binnen is gebruikt en die het geheel een moderne, industriële uitstraling geven.

100% Interior

Am Botanischen Garten 18
D-50735 Cologne–Germany
T: +49 221 736383
F: +49 221 736318
interior@netcologne.de
www.100interior.de

24H Architecture

Van Nelleweg 1206
3004 BC Rotterdam–the Netherlands
T: +31 10 7503 150
F: +31 10 7503 160
info@24h-architecture.com
www.24h-architecture.com

3deluxe

Schwalbacherstraße 74
D-65183 Wiesbaden–Germany
T: +49 611 95 22 05-28
F: +49 611 95 22 05-22
m.reusch@3deluxe.de
www.3deluxe.de

II by IV Design Associates

77 Mowat Avenue, Suite 109
Toronto, ON M6K 3E3–Canada
T: +1 416 531 2224
F: +1 416 642 0102
www.iibyiv.com

A Prima

Rambla Catalunya 127, ático 1ª
08008 Barcelona–Spain
T: +34 93 415 86 35
F: +34 93 441 22 02
aprimadisseny@terra.es
www.crom-interdis.com

Adam Tihany

135 West 27th Street, 9th Floor
New York, NY 10001–United States
T: +1 212 366 5544
F: +1 212 366 4302
mail@tihanydesign.com
www.tihanydesign.com

Alonso Balaguer

Bac de Roda 40
08019 Barcelona–Spain
T: +34 93 303 4160
F: +34 93 303 4161
estudi@alonsobalaguer.com
www.alonsobalaguer.com

Amalgam

23 Old Street
London EC1V 9HG–United Kingdom
T: +44 20 7250 4123
F: +44 20 7250 4126
margery.craig@amalgam.co.uk
www.amalgam.co.uk

Andrea Viviani

Via Fra' Eremitano 12
35138 Padova–Italy
T: +39 049 661461
F: +39 049 8756776
www.andreaviviani.it
a.viviani@awn.it

Aranda Pigem Vilalta Arquitectes

Passeig de Blay 34, 2.
17800 Olot–Spain
T: +34 972 26 91 05
F: +34 972 26 75 58
rcr.arquitectes@coac.es
www.rcrarquitectes.es

Architectenbureau Van den Broek en Bakema

Postbus 13084, 3004HB Rotterdam
van Nelleweg 1, 3044BC Rotterdam–
the Netherlands
T: +31 10 413 47 80
F: +31 10 413 64 54
broekbakema@broekbakema.nl
www.broekbakema.nl

Atelier Van Lieshout

Keilestraat 43e
3029 BP Rotterdam–the Netherlands
T: +31 10 244 09 71
F: +31 10 244 09 72
info@ateliervanlieshout.com
www.ateliervanlieshout.com

Avante UK

Thistle House, Thistle Way
Gildersome Spur, Gildersome, Morley
Leeds LS27 7JZ–United Kingdom
T: +44 113 201 2240
www.avantebathrooms.com

Bisazza

Viale Milano 56
36041 Alte di Montecchio – Italy
T: +39 044 707511
F:+ 39 044 492088
www.bisazza.com

Bolzen, Mehring & Partner

Süchteler Strasse 42
D-41066 Mönchengladbach–Germany
T: +49 2161 24 88 78-0
F: +49 2161 24 88 78-1
info@architekten-bmp.de
www.architekten-bmp.de

Bothe Richter Teherani

Oberbaumbrücke 1
D20457 Hamburg–Germany
T: +49 40 24 84 2-205
F: +49 40 24 84 2-222
a.stueper@brt.de

Brunete Fraccaroli

Rua Guarará, 261, 7° andar Jd. Paulista
01425-001 São Paulo–Brazil
T: +11 3885 8309
brunete@osite.com.br
www.brunetefraccaroli.com.br

Buckley Gray Yeoman

Studio 5.04
The Tea Building
56 Shoreditch High Street
London E1 6JJ–United Kingdom
T: +44 20 7033 9913
F: +44 20 7033 9914
www.buckleygrayyeoman.com
mail@buckleygrayyeoman.com

Camenzind Evolution

Samariterstrasse 5, Postfach
CH-8030 Zurich–Switzerland
T: +41 44 253 9500
F: +41 44 253 9510
info@CamenzindEvolution.com
http://www.CamenzindEvolution.com

Capilla Vallejo Arquitectos

Monasterio de Cilveti 4
31011 Pamplona - España
T: +34 948 274316
F: +34 948 171280
estudio@cvarquitectos.es
www.cvarquitectos.es

Carlos Ferrater

Balmes, 379
Barcelona–Spain
T: +34 93 418 8539
cart@coac.es

Claudio Silvestrin Architects

Unit 412 Kingswharf
301 Kingsland Road
London E8 4DS–United Kingdom
T: +44 20 7275 7515
F: +44 20 7275 0762
c.silvestrin@claudiosilvestrin.com
www.claudiosilvestrin.com

Concrete Architectural Associates

Rozengracht 133 III
1016 LV Amsterdam–the Netherlands
T. +31 20 52 00 200
F. +31 20 52 00 201
info@concrete.archined.nl
www.concrete.archined.nl

CZWG

17 Bowling Green Lane
London EC1R 0QB–United Kingdom
T: +44 20 7253 2523
mail@czwgarchitects.co.uk

David Collins

6-7 Chelsea Wharf, Lots Road
London SW10 0QJ–United Kingdom
T: +44 20 7349 5900
F: +44 20 7352 7284
studio@davidcollins.com
www.davidcollins.com

Desgrippes Gobé Group

411 Lafayette St.
New York NY 10014–United States
T: +1 212 979 8900
info@dga.com
http://www.dga.com

Designrichtung

Luisenstrasse 25
CH-8005 Zürich–Switzerland
T: +41 44 422 53 20
F: +41 44 422 53 27
hindermann@designrichtung.ch

Eichinger oder Knechtl

Franzjosefskai 29
A-1010 Vienna–Austria
T: +43 1 535 54 24
F: +43 1 535 40 39
desk@eok.at
www.eok.at

Fabio Novembre

Via Mecenate 76
Milan–Italy
T: +39 2 504 104
info@novembre.it
www.novembre.it

Feuring Hotelconsulting GmbH

An der Karlsschanze 8
55131 Mainz–Germany
T: +49 6131 98 222 89
www.feuring.com

Fòrum de las Culturas

Llull 95-97 planta 6
08005 Barcelona–Spain
T: +34 93 320 90 10
F: +34 93 489 89 05
media@barcelona2004.org

Francesc Rifé

Escoles Pies, 25 Baixos
08017 Barcelona–Spain
T: +34 93 414 12 88
F: +34 93 241 28 14
f@rife-design.com

Freeland Rees Roberts Architects

25 City Road
Cambridge CB1 1DP–United Kingdom
T: +44 1223 366 555
F: +44 1223 312 882
info@frrarchitects.co.uk
www.frrarchitects.co.uk

Fumita Design Office

2-18-2 Minami Aoyama
Minato ku, Tokyo 107-0062–Japan
T: +81 3 5414 2880
F: +81 3 5414 2881
mail@fumitadesign.com
www.fumitadesign.com

GAD Architecture

9 Desbrosses Street
New York, NY 10013–United States
T: +1 917 679 4971
F: +1 212 941 6496
gadny@gadarchitecture.com
www.gadarchitecture.com

Gasparin & Meier

10. Oktoberstrasse 18
A-9500 Villach–Austria
T: +43 4242 22061 0
F: +43 4242 22061 1
arch.g@gasparinmeier.at
www.gasparinmeier.at

Greg Burgess

104 Burwood Road
Hawthorn. Victoria 3122–Australia
T: +2 03 9818 0335
F: +2 03 9818 3017
gba@gregaryburgessarchitects.com.au

Harper Mackay

33-37 Charterhouse Square
London EC1M 6EA–United Kingdom
T: +44 20 7600 5151
F: +44 20 7600 1092
www.harpermackay.com

Herzog & De Meuron

Rheinschanze 6
4056 Basel–Switzerland
T: +41 61 385 57 58
F: +41 61 385 57 57

Jakob + MacFarlane

13 rue des petites Ecuries
Paris–France
T: +33 1 4479 0572
jakmak@club-internet.fr

Jasmax with Mario Madayag Architecture

65 Upper Queen St
Box 6648 Auckland–New Zealand
T: +64 9 366 9626
F: +64 9 366 9629
www.jasmax.com

Jestico + Whiles

1 Cobourg Street
London NW1 2HP–United Kingdom
T: +44 20 7380 0382
F: +44 20 7380 0511
j+w@jesticowhiles.co.uk
www.jesticowhiles.co.uk

John Friedman Alice Kimm Architects

701 East Third Street, Suite 300
Los Angeles, CA 90013-1843–United States
T: +1 213 253 4740
F: +1 213 253 4760
jfak@jfak.net
www.jfak.net

Karim Rashid Design

357 West 17th St.
New York, NY 10011–United States
T: +1 212 929 8657
F: +1 212 929 0247
office@karimrashid.com
www.karimrashid.com

Kristian Gavoille

220 rue du Faubourg Saint-Martin
75010 Paris–France
T: +33 1 42 09 42 42
F: +33 1 42 09 42 44
kristiangavoille@freesurf.fr
www.kristiangavoille.com

Lacock Gullam

Oblique Workshops
Stamford Works, Gillett Street
London N16 8JH–United Kingdom
T: +44 20 7503 4001
studio@lacockgullam.co.uk

Leonardo Anecca

53 rue Montreuil
75011 Paris–France
T: +33 1 444 99006
leonardo@l-a-design.com

Lifschutz Davidson

Thames Wharf Studios
Rainville Road
London W6 9HA–United Kingdom
T: +44 20 7381 8120
F: +44 20 7385 3118
info@lifschutzdavidson.com
www.lifschutzdavidson.com

Marcelo Sodré

Rua Salvador Corrêa 628
18030-130 Sorocaba, Sao Paulo–Brazil
sodre@splicenet.com.br
www.marcelosodre.com.br

Ma,Piva

Via Maiocchi 9
20129 Milano–Italy
T: +39 0229 400 814
pm.tender2@libero.it
www.studiomarcopiva.it

Massimiliano Fuksas

Piazza del Monte di Pieta 30
I-00186 Rome–Italy
T: +39 6 6880 7871
office@fuksas.it
www.fu4sas.it

Matali Crasset Productions

26 rue du buisson Saint Louis
75010 Paris–France
T: +33 1 42 40 99 89
F: +33 1 42 40 99 98
matali.crasset@wanadoo.fr
www.matalicrasset.com

Matteo Thun

Via Appiani 9
I-20121 Milan–Italy
T: +39 02 655691
F: +39 02 6570646
info@matteothun.com
www.matteothun.com

Maurizio Lai

Via Settala 6
20124 Milan–Italy
T: +39 02 89059907
F: +39 02 89059545
lai1@lai-studio.com
www.lai-studio.com

MMW Studio34

Schweigaardsgt.34 d
N-0191 Oslo–Norway
T: +47 22 17 34 40
F: + 47 22 17 34 41
mail@mmw.no
www.mmw.no

Monica Bonvicini

c/o Galleria Emi Fontana
Viale Bligny 42
20136 Milan–Italy
T: +39 02 5832 2237
F: +39 02 5830 6855
emif@micronet.it

Mourad Mazouz

9 Conduit Street
Mayfair, London W1–United Kingdom
T: +44 870 777 44 88
F: +44 207 629 1684
www.sketch.uk.com

Nenad Fabijanic

Cvjetna Cesta 9
10000 Zagreb–Croatia
T: +385 1 4639230
F: +385 1 4639349

Nicholas Grimshaw & Partners

1 Conaway Street, Fitzroy Square
London W1P 6LR–United Kingdom
T: +44 20 7291 4141
F: +44 20 7291 4194
communications@grimshaw-architects.com
www.ngrimshaw.co.uk

Noé Duchaufour-Lawrence

8 Passage de la Bonne Graine
75 011 Paris–France
T: +33 1 43 14 99 59
F: +33 1 43 14 48 68
noe@neonata.fr

Office dA

57 East Concord Street 6
Boston, Massachusetts 02118–
United States
T: +1 617 267 7369
F: +1 617 859 4948
da@officeda.com

OMA

Heer Bokelweg 149
NL 3032 AD Rotterdam–the Netherlands
T: +31 10 2438200
F: +31 10 2438202
pr@OMA.nl

Phillippe Starck

18-20 rue du Faubourg du Temple
75011 Paris–France
T: +33 1 48 07 54 54
F: +33 1 48 07 54 64
starck@starckdesign.com
www.philippe-starck.com

Pilots Product Design

Entrepotdok 164
1018 AD Amsterdam–the Netherlands
T: +31 20 420 13 33
jop@pilotsdesign.nl
www.pilotsdesign.com

Propeller Z

Mariahilferstrasse 101/ 3/ 55
1060 Vienna–Austria
T: +43 1 595 2727 0
F: +43 1 595 2727 27
mail@propellerz.at
www.propellerz.at

RHWL Architects

77 Endell Street
London WC2H 9DZ–United Kingdom
T: +44 20 7379 7900
F: +44 20 7836 4881
ysumner@rhwl.co.uk
www.rhwl.co.uk

Rüdiger Lainer

Bellariastrasse 12
A-1010 Vienna–Austria
T: +43 1 522 3922 0
F: +43 1 522 3922 43
architect@lainer.at
www.lainer.at

Satmoko Ball Architecture Design

21d Bradbury Mews, Bradbury Street
London N16 8JW–United Kingdom
T: +44 20 7254 5200
F: +44 20 7254 0059
studio@satmokoball.co.uk
www.satmokoball.co.uk

Simone Micheli

Via Aretina 197 r/ 199 r/ 201 r
50136 Florence–Italy
T: +39 055 691 216
F: +39 055 650 4498
simone@simonemicheli.com
www.simonemicheli.com

Studio Gallucci

Via dei Quattro Cantoni 58
00184 Rome–Italy
T: +39 06 489 30 045
studiogallucci@studiogallucci.it
www.studiogallucci.it

Ulla Blennemann

Bilker Str. 28
40213 Düsseldorf–Germany
T: +49 211 157 60 69 0
F: +49 211 157 60 69 9
info@ubhome.de

Urban Salon

Unit D, Flat Iron Yard
Ayres Street
London SE1 1ES–United Kingdom
T: +44 20 7357 8800
F: +44 20 7407 2800
mail@urbansalonarchitects.com
www.urbansalonarchitects.com

Wilkinson Eyre Architects

Transworld House
100 City Road
London EC14 2BP–United Kingdom
T: +44 20 76 08 79 00
F: +44 20 76 08 79 01
info@wilkinsoneyre.com
www.wilkinsoneyre.com

Will Bruder Architects

111 West Monroe, Suite 444
Phoenix, AZ 85003 – United States
T: +1 602 324 6012
F. +1 602 324 6001
www.willbruder.com